MW00975013

How I Learned To Smile From The Inside

Seth E Santoro CEC

How I Learned To Smile From The Inside

Seth E Santoro CEC

A Smile From The Inside Production ☺
Los Angeles, CA

Copyright © 2013 Seth E Santoro CEC
All rights reserved.

ISBN: 1478319232

ISBN 13: 9781478319238

A Smile From The Inside Production ☺

DEDICATION

I dedicate this book to Mom and Dad for their unwavering support and love in every decision I have made over the years…including the good as well as the not so good.

TABLE OF CONTENTS

INTRODUCTION

When you have lost your smile, what do you do? How will you find it again?

Why You Need to Know This Now?

I want you to find your smile again... and pronto! Life is tough! There is no way around that. Lately, everywhere I turn, there is sadness, violence, and anger. It's so easy to get caught up in the negative, the gnarly and believe in all the cynicism that exists around us. By the time I was thirty-two years old, I had almost died twice and been through a great deal of trauma and unexpected events. I searched all around for something to help me. I started doing research. I could not find what I was looking for...

so I wrote it. Now, I want to share my Smile From The Inside approach and S.M.I.L.E. Method with the world.

People would rather be happy than be sad. When you are unhappy, life seems like such a chore and so heavy. When you are happy, life is a gift, it's fun, and you get to play. There's no time like the present.

In all of my research, I have found that there are only two types of feelings in the world - those that are on the positive side: happiness, joy, enthusiasm, passion; and those that are on the negative side: sadness, grief, anger, etc. Someone who Smiles From The Inside feels more feelings from the positive side. It is time for us to change cynicism into hope and affirmation. It is time for us to shift the world consciousness from sadness, violence, and anger into contentment, peace, and giving. This is not an easy task, but it is a possible one. One by one, by being the example we wish to see, we can affect change - starting at home with our families, in the workplace, in our respective towns and cities, and beyond. Let's all walk the walk and talk the talk.

Smiling From The Inside

Smiling From The Inside is a lifestyle choice. It is not a state of mind - it is a way of being. Smiling From The Inside will help you breathe a little deeper, walk a little taller, and run a little faster. It's living a more centered and balanced experience. Self-awareness is key to this choice of lifestyle. The more aware you are, the more authentic you can be, the more confidence you carry within, and the more efficiently you can deal with issues that come up. The bottom line is that we all want an easier go at life and we all want a more enjoyable life. If you follow the lessons, instructions, and suggestions herein and learn from some of my crazy and life-dizzying experiences, it will make your life easier and bring you more joy... now.

You may be curious as to what people who Smile From The Inside look like. Well, they look just like you and me. When they smile, however, their way of being shines through so brightly, it is impossible not to notice the depth, the hope, and the happiness within. It means that they are mostly happy people. That said, the majority of the time, you will not only see the truth, giving, and joy but also the enthusiastic life energy, motivation, and empowerment through their smile alone.

Life sucks sometimes. Right now may be one of those times. For the most part, life rocks too! Life can be the most beautiful thing you will ever know or, within an instant, it can sneak up on you and be the ugliest thing ever! Life is a complete inside-out and upside-down experience. It can rock us to the core in happiness and push us to the outer edges of utter disappointment. I fully believe in the idea that the more creative and amazing your thoughts and feelings are at all times, the more amazing and creative your time here will be. Thank you for having picked up or downloaded this book. I *know* it will help you.

One of the first questions you may be asking yourself after an unexpected or tragic event occurs is, "Why me? What did I do to deserve this?" I've asked myself these questions many, many times. These are the questions we ask ourselves when it just does not make sense, or we just cannot wrap our minds around the event. Right now, it sucks. Sometimes, there are no words to describe what goes on in our minds or hearts. Sometimes we cannot find the right words to express ourselves. There are also times when the words are there, we know how we feel, yet we cannot actually verbalize our hearts' aches. Maybe someone important is no longer physically around, for whatever reason – it could be a break-up, or the passing of a loved one, or the person is no longer speaking to you... It is difficult, lousy, and you are probably finding it even hard to breathe.

This book is intended to help people who have somehow lost their smile. You just received really bad news at work, just lost the love of your life, or found out you might lose the love of your life. It could be you have just lost a loved one or a pet... anything shocking to the core. Be it for health-related reasons, financial troubles, relationship issues, family troubles, or work-related issues, you got some really bad news. Okay, now what do you do? Where do you go from this point? How the hell did you get here? What exactly is going on? These are typical questions you may be asking yourself, but there are many more. Whatever just happened to you, it sucks! If you are in one of those spaces, or just came out of that space, this book is for you.

Who am I?

I'm Seth Santoro! Why should you listen to me? I was completely ill-prepared for all of the unexpected and tragic events that have occurred to me in recent years. I have always been a thinker, analyzer, and processor. Being well versed in all things trauma, I had to complete my own investigations and find what worked for me. I analyzed the present as well as the past, considered all options, and, lastly, drew my own conclusions. I have put all of this into a concise and easy-to-follow format, a sort of one-stop shop. I have done all the work for you and am therefore saving you time. In the end, I figured, if it worked for me, it could work for others.

The vision for my life is to **Inspire the World, One By One, To Smile From The Inside**. I am a spiritual philanthropist, of sorts. Right now, instead of giving money, I give smiles, insight, and love. No matter where I am - in line at WalMart, on an airplane, anywhere, really - if I feel someone is in need of a smile, I will never miss a chance to furnish one. I want other people to smile. It takes a deep understanding, awareness, and commitment to Smile From The Inside, but we all have the capacity to inspire and encourage people to smile. We have to start somewhere, right?

I have been formally trained as a Certified Empowerment Coach by the Institute for Professional Excellence in Coaching (IPEC) and I am a registered Professional Coach with the International Coaching Federation (coachfederation.org). You may call me a Life Coach or a Life Expert. You could call me the gay Dr. Phil, a Life Strategist, or you could call me an old soul, like my mother does. I like to think I am a mensch. "Mensch" is an amazing Yiddish word meaning a person of integrity and honor. To some, I am a hero, a spiritual warrior, a healer. I have even been called an angel, which I will tell you about... all in good time, dear friend.

I am a Reframer. What is a Reframer?

When you reframe something, you change how people view a particular conflict to allow for different tactics and approaches to that conflict, or you help guide other people to look at, present, or think of their beliefs, ideas, or relationships in a new and/or different way. There is a particularly interesting concept referred to as "Cognitive

Reframing," which is "a technique by which a person learns to stop his or her negative thought process and replace the negative thoughts with more positive self-talk," (Phobias.About.com)[1] or "a psychotherapy technique that teaches people to think differently about the challenges they face" (Center for Advanced Health)[2].

For my purposes here, a Reframer encompasses the following: an intuitive individual who inspires and encourages others to shift their limited views, actions, and/or behaviors, by dealing with the past, healing in the present, and reeling/wheeling into the future, all in an effort to achieve the ultimate in self-expression, Smiling From The Inside.

I look just like you. I am "a spiritual being having a human experience," as my own Life Coach, Lynne Goldberg, would always say. Other than that, I'm a regular New England-born/bred gay boy with a hell of a lot to say, an incredible/infinite amount of passion and endless enthusiasm, as you will see. You can choose to do some of the action-oriented methods that I suggest, or not. It is all up to you. All I ask is that you are open to anything I might say, no matter how weird, uncomfortable, or terrible it sounds.

Over the past decade or so, I have endured a lifetime's worth of experiences. I have survived aggressive skin cancer. I narrowly escaped contracting HIV from an unfaithful partner. I lived through the horrors of 9/11 in Manhattan. Four good friends passed away, and I lost two dogs all within the span of three years. Last, but certainly not least, I was almost kidnapped in Mexico.

---

1   "Cognitive Reframing," Phobias.About.com, 2012.

2   "Cognitive Reframing," CFAH.com, 2012.

Because of these experiences, I have all of the reasons in the world to be a depressed, sad individual, but I have done a great deal of work on myself, I believe in myself and I will never give up, ever! I will speak about how each of these circumstances has broadened my life and inspired me to grow and heal. We're not reaching for Nirvana here, just to Smile From The Inside!

From time to time, I like to invent useful words when nothing in the dictionary names perfectly my meaning. I sometimes feel the need to editorialize, make comments, and digress from time to time, but I assure you, I always circle back to the topic at hand. I write just like a conversation amongst friends, so remember to take breaths as you read. If you like what you read here, tell every-body, so that we can spread the joy of Smiling From The Inside!

The Extraordinary Life of an Extraordinary Woman: Dr. Elisabeth Kübler-Ross

You may or may not be familiar with the individual behind the Five Stages of Loss. Without her incredible dedication to the pro-cess of inspiring life by confronting death, this manuscript would not have been possible. Her work has not only inspired me, but also has inspired countless generations of psychologists, self-help writers, and psychiatrists.

Dr. Kübler-Ross was an extremely accomplished psychiatrist. Her most famous book, *On Death and Dying*, published in 1969, is where her Five Stages of Grief are first introduced to the world of psycho-analytics, as a pattern of adjustment. The five stages, as she saw them, are Denial, Anger, Bargaining, Depression, and Acceptance. For over forty years, scholars of psychology have embraced these phases of grief/loss which she outlined. I am now giving those Five Stages of Loss a makeover in *How I Learned to Smile From The Inside*.

Over the course of thirty-four years, Dr. Kübler-Ross published twenty-three manuscripts, which have been translated into over thirty languages. She founded the American Holistic Medical Association and received over twenty honorary degrees from various universities and private institutions throughout the world. She has been awarded the following distinguished honors: Woman of the Year Award, *Ladies Home Journal*, 1977; Women of the Decade, *Ladies Home Journal*, 1979; One Hundred Most Important Thinkers of the Century, *Time Magazine*, 1999; Honorary Inductee into the National Women's Hall of Fame, 2007. Unfortunately, on August 24, 2004, in Scottsdale, Arizona, the triplet who pioneered the medical practices on dying and grieving passed away.[3]

Dr. Kübler-Ross changed the landscape of analytical thought on grieving and loss forever. It was due to her revolutionary work that therapists and medical practitioners around the globe transformed their patient understanding, bedside manners, and medical practices for dying patients and grieving families. Dr. Elisabeth definitely made quite an impact on the medical, hospice, and psychiatric realms and deserves nothing but the utmost respect and admiration from everyone. Personally, I found her approach precise, concise, easy to understand, and easy to follow. I have used those qualities to develop my own approach.

---

3   ekrfoundation.org

How This Book Works!

This book is divided into five sections explained below: the Five Stages of Healing. To better explain each stage of healing, I share five very personal stories of my own and take you on my emotional healing journey through the five stages. My S.M.I.L.E. model focuses on dealing with any recent unexpected, traumatic, or sad events. The S.M.I.L.E. approach helps people gain awareness and a deep understanding of their individual healing process, which occurs directly following trauma or unexpected news of any type. I believe that everyone can heal. I believe that everyone experiences his or her own journey to healing, similarly, if not identically, to the S.M.I.L.E. model set forth in this book. Keep that in mind as you continue reading.

I am going to teach you all you need to know about the S.M.I.L.E. Method for healing, essential for living a Smile From the Inside way of life. I am not only going to share my personal stories, and recommend ideas to keep in mind, but I am also going to offer analogies to help cement these concepts into your mind. For example, I find that the S.M.I.L.E. Method for healing is almost identical to the five inherent parts of a 21st century yoga class. Within each chapter, I will succinctly deconstruct each concept in the S.M.I.L.E. Method to show you how it correlates to the five major sections within a yoga class: warm-up; practice and conditioning; stretching your limits; learning to balance; and Savasana (dead corpse pose).

Keep the following thought in your mind: **pain is inevitable, but suffering is optional**!

The Five Stages of Healing

S.   Shock

M.   Mock-cceptance

I.   In Overwhelmdom

L.   Learning

E.   Embrace

First - We explore the richness and variety of initial **Shock**. **Shock** is nature's first line of defense in protecting the mind, body, and soul.

Second - Denial is bliss in the form of **Mock-cceptance,** which is part-denial, part-acceptance. Whilst in blissful denial, we have a period of "**Mock-cceptance**", or denied acceptance, where it might even feel at times that all is well and you are dealing with the issue. In actuality, your mind is playing a trick on your heart without you realizing it.

Third - **In Overwhelmdom**. Ouch! This is otherwise referred to as anger and depression. This part sucks. This part hurts. This part is the part that no one wishes upon anyone else (well… at least we shouldn't). This is where the hurricane of emotions hit you. It is challenging, but you *will* get through it.

Fourth - **Learning**. I love this word. This is the final exploration of sadness and truth in an attempt to understand what's going on. This is when we realize that even though we don't want things to change, they do and they have already. We start to learn from our mistakes and begin to move forward.

Fifth - **Embrace**. Congratulations! This is where you accept and evolve. This is where the freedom begins and the dance of life continues.

Please note that some thoughts laid out here are more pragmatic than others, and some are indeed esoteric. I believe that the ideas and notions that follow will speak to all people who have been wise or fortunate enough to pick up this book. The thoughts and messages herein are my little violet gems (violet is my favorite color) in which everyone can partake.

Lastly, if, as Howard Bragman, Hollywood P.R. agent, says, Oprah is all about enlightenment and empowerment, Dr. Phil is about redemption, and Ellen is about originality and freshness, then Seth Santoro is all about SMILING FROM THE INSIDE!

Are you ready to find your smile again? Enjoy *How I Learned To Smile From The Inside*....

THE S.M.I.L.E. MODEL

The purpose of this book is to apply the S.M.I.L.E. approach to your life so you may Smile From The Inside. Remember from the introduction that the S.M.I.L.E. approach helps people gain awareness and a deep understanding of their individual healing process, which occurs *directly following* trauma or unexpected news of any type. If you didn't read the introduction, shame on you! Really, though, go back and read it.

Five Stages of Healing in the S.M.I.L.E Model	
SHOCK	"Whoa!" or "I'm sorry, what?" - Shock is nature's first line of protection, the buffer, and defense to protect the mind, body, and soul.
MOCK-CCEPTANCE	"I'm fine!" or "Why do I feel so good?" - Part-Denial, Part-Acceptance.
IN OVERWHELMDOM	"Ugh!" or "Why am I so emotional right now?" - Anger. Sadness. Overall irritation and emotionality toward everything! The truth is settling in now.
LEARNING	"Ohhh… Wow!" - That was some ride. Now, I get to comprehend what happened, my responsibility in it, and how I will handle the situation much differently next time.
EMBRACE	"Yeehaw!" - I have enthusiastically accepted that which has happened to me and I am ready to smile again.

SHOCK

STAGE ONE: SHOCK.
Shock

noun

1. A disturbance in the equilibrium or permanence of something, or a sudden or violent mental or emotional disturbance[1].

2. Any sudden or unexpected experience of extreme surprise, horror, or outrage; any violent impact or jarring.

3. In medical discourse, another name for "traumatic shock"[2].

---

1   "Shock," Merriam-Webster Dictionary, 2012.

2   "Shock," Colman, Andrew M., Oxford Dictionary of Psychology. Oxford University Press, 2009.

Traumatic Shock

noun

1. The partial or total collapse of voluntary and involuntary bodily functions resulting from circulatory failure or a sudden drop in blood pressure, brought about by physical trauma, especially blood loss or injury to the spinal cord, anaphylaxis, or intense psychological trauma or stress[3].

Expressed Feeling = "Whoa!"

What is **Shock** anyway? Above is what the experts have to say. **Traumatic Shock** is right in line with my own personal feeling about the concept. I believe that the state of **Shock** is nature's first line of defense when an overwhelming blow or surprising event occurs without warning. Sometimes the human mind, body, and soul cannot process the plethora of information coming in from said experience and they attempt to put everything on hold. **Shock** results from the incapability to utilize the five senses to receive or process the surprising or upsetting information. It takes your breath away. It can cause dizziness. Be careful. Do NOT operate any heavy machinery when in **Shock**. It is like a computer asking if you are sure you want to restart... only the answer is on automatic.

Shock is the mind's way of saying, "**Whoa!** Wait a second! This cannot be real! Oh, my God, is this really happening?" **Shock** is a much-needed blockage. In my opinion, it temporarily prevents the onset of **Overwhelmdom**. **Shock** is the

---

3 "Traumatic Shock," Colman, Andrew M., Oxford Dictionary of Psychology. Oxford University Press, 2009.

body's way of preventing an overload to the mind and heart for just long enough to let the brain process the event, slowly and at its very own pace. It allows us the space we need to understand just what is going on or what has just happened. The mind is an amazing thing; it plays these tricks on us as a survival mechanism. Sometimes we need a huge blockage; other times not so much. It all depends on the situation confronting you at the time. **Shock** is there to protect us and shield us from an emotional and physical overload.

Here are some small words of wisdom for anyone in this state of surprise. Nature knows what she is doing! You won't break. It might feel like it, but you won't. Trust me. I've had my share of receptor information overload. Take three deep breaths. Take a deep breath in. Exhale. Second, take another breath in. Exhale. And third, take one more breath… and… exhale… I find that three deep breaths always helps me to come back to the present moment. You are not alone. As alone as you may feel at times, we are never truly alone. Always remember to take care of yourself, and straight away. Be gentle, patient and nice with yourself. Remember to give time a little time and take things slowly. Be honest with where you are now and how you feel. Be yourself… even if yourself is not very nice.

Call your best friends to come over (but not people who think that by filling the void with their voices that they will help you in any way). Tell them to expect nothing. Tell them you just need someone to sit with you, watch television with you, be with you, and perhaps even hold your hand. If you are the friend, remain silent and just sit there with them. Remember, laughter always helps. Do not drag on about your problems. Don't mention anything at all about why you are there, unless they bring it up. You are there to just be there. So just be there. Talk to them. Listen to them. And that's all.

Most people think that **Shock** is a bad thing, something to be avoided. I believe it is a positive first step in overcoming overwhelming obstacles. You will soon discover that understanding the value and purpose of **Shock** is essential to living a fuller and happier Smile-From-The-Inside existence. Think about **Shock** as the warm-up exercises for your mind and body, just like in a yoga class. And, if you listen to the following stories, you will learn how **Shock** plays a fundamental role in the S.M.I.L.E. Method for healing.

Um... You Lost Me at Cancer

My mother was always concerned with our health. There is an old Jewish saying, "Wear it or use it in the best of health" which my mother always used say to us, when we got a new outfit or after being given a present. It is a very sweet saying. It is also very Jewish. I never realized just how important my health was to me until I was diagnosed with Superficial Spreading Malignant Melanoma. Say that ten times fast. It is quite the doozy!

Let me back up just a little. In December of 2005, seven months prior to being diagnosed, I moved straight across the United States from New York City to Los Angeles. It was mostly prompted by a relationship break-up and a thirst for success in the Hollywood entertainment realm.

It was a very hard time for me. At first, I lived in a crumby apartment with some type of bug infestation in a very sketchy neighborhood. I finally moved into a beautifully clean apartment with two wonderful people in a glorious neighborhood. Ryan, one of my roommates, was obsessed with health, especially with skin health. He went to this fabulous, high profile Beverly Hills dermatology center and encouraged all of his friends to go and get checked out.

After some months of hesitation, I finally caved and went to see his dermatologist. I was not nervous at all, to be honest. I never thought that anything would be wrong with my test results. All in all, they removed about ten moles. With each mole removed, biopsies were done to ensure that they were, in fact, benign. The majority of the moles were diagnosed as dysplastic nevi, which are pre-pre-pre cancerous cells. Needless to say, that was scary enough for me. After a few weeks of the same results, I became blah about the test results. Never, ever, did I think I would be diagnosed with cancer?

It was a Monday evening at about 6pm when I received the phone call from the dermatologist's assistant. The conversation might have been routine and no big deal for her – however, for me, it was life changing. She advised me in a very nonchalant manner, "I got your results. Now, you did come back with a superficial spreading malignant melanoma. So I would like you to come in again right away. We are going to refer you to the oncologist associated with our office. He happens to be the best skin cancer surgeon on the West Coast. If you are going to go to anyone, we highly recommend that you go to him. Would you like his number?"

Perhaps to her, it seemed like just another regular, everyday phone conversation, but not to me. I had to sit down. Ok… in my mind, I know what malignant means. I mean in this day and age, who doesn't? As coincidence would have it (turns out not really much of a coincidence at all), I did my 8th grade science project on skin cancer, so I knew it was the most common cancer. For the life of me, though, I could not figure out what "superficial spreading" meant. To me, that sounded horrible. I was so **Shock**ed that I do not even think I said anything. I heard her say, "Hello?" I said, "Yeah. I'm sorry. Did you say I have melanoma? I know what malignant means and I know what melanoma means. What does superficial spreading mean?"

She responded (are you ready for this?), "Oh yeah, it's the number one most deadly cancer of all cancers. I'm really glad we caught it as early as we did!" She advised me to call the oncologist's office right away and make an appointment.

Again, I was just stunned. I said, "Ok... you lost me at melanoma. Let's go through this again. And what stage am I? Who's this oncologist?" The words barely could come out of my mouth. I don't think I had ever used the word "oncologist" before with regard to anyone else, let alone with regard to myself. Who knew that it would become an extremely important word for the rest of my life.

She explained everything to me again, this time with a little bit of irritation in her voice. I let it slide that day, but you better believe that I told her later on that I thought her "bedside manner" was poor and she should have a bit more compassion while telling people they have cancer. The normal layperson would not understand the severity or non-severity of the situation until someone explained it to him, which in this case, was me.

I was still stunned. I tried to gather as much information as possible, but she really had lost me at "cancer". I stammered out a few questions, and tried to listen to her answers, but it was hard to take in her words, because I was in **Shock**. I do remember her explaining to me that once the oncologist received the biopsy, it would take him an additional three to four days to do his intensive studies and decide what the best course of action would be.

After we hung up the phone, I just sat down on my bed and numbed out for about fifteen minutes. I have cancer. I have cancer. I have cancer... just kept going through my mind. I was numb. What probably was three minutes felt more like an hour of normal human time. Since I had no idea how sick or what stage I was, I really could not pinpoint a feeling for you. I was null of feelings and void of anything. A great wave of sadness and weight fell upon my heart.

Within a few minutes, however, I felt okay and I felt ready to do whatever I needed to do in my life, such as chemotherapy, radiation, or surgery. No matter what I was about to face, I knew I had the inner strength to do it.

I realized I had to call my parents and let them know. Then my mind produced a whole list of people with whom I would need to share my news. In addition to my parents, I had to call my sister, then my ex, then my aunt, my roommates, my close friends, my boss, etc... It was the first thing I could think of to do.

It was not clear to me how to break the bad news to Mom and Dad. I had to make sure that I could get the words out. When I finally mustered the courage to call them, they were more stunned than I was. I know everyone deals with receiving devastating news differently; their **Shock** lasted about two minutes until the fury of questions commenced. I did not know the answers to most of their questions. It was an extremely tough conversation with them. The only thing I could focus on was what was next, who was next, and what was I going to do with my remaining time left? I know, I know… a bit dramatic… but all of those thoughts were definitely going through my mind at warp speed.

Within 24 hours, I met this amazing oncologist. He sat down with me face-to-face. He spoke slowly and calmly. He looked me in the eyes when he spoke, which was very reassuring.

I asked a good friend from work to accompany me… because you should always, ALWAYS take someone else with you for those types of appointments. They can be scary, intimidating and downright wretched. And, I guarantee that you will only get about 50% of what the physician tells you anyway, so by having the additional person with you, they can advise you later of the parts that you missed.

This amazing surgeon explained the process of what was going to happen, one day at a time, and all of the next steps. He very gently pointed out that I had to wait three days for his office to perform a more comprehensive biopsy of the mole/skin that was already removed. Those were the three longest and saddest days of my life. Once the results were in, we could make decisions about chemo, surgery, radiation, etc… His bedside manner was impeccable, honest, and sincere. He walked me through all of the options, and appeared optimistic. So, I went with it!

I am usually really good in emergency or urgent situations. I always have a plan B or, if not, I can create one fast. With this situation, all I could do was plan and get organized. For me, the **Shock** lasted about 72 hours. It was **Shock**, coupled with extreme emotion, prior to the **Mock-cceptance** stage.

To Be Continued...

I Thought We Were Monogamous!

I thought we were monogamous!!! I mean, you know, the occasional three-way, but NEVER without each other. Ahem... I guess I was wrong.

Fast forward to August of 2010. For those of you who do not know what sero-conversion means, it is when one goes from an HIV negative status to an HIV positive status (or a positive status for any immunodeficiency disease). I had been seeing this really fantastic and sexy Italian guy, Paolo, for about fifteen months or so when he sero-converted. Please note "Paolo" is a fictitious name.

I thought things were going well for about a year. And, then, as the months progressed, our intimacy started to go downhill... and fast. It appeared that the closer we got to each other, the more problems with intimacy he started having. And, as some of you may know, people with intimacy issues can usually have sex with many different people (no judgments at all) except the person with whom they have the "budding" relationship. Sound familiar, anyone? This may be an interesting thought for the majority of you. Let me explain. It appears that for those individuals who had a very heavy childhood with abandonment or similar experiences, or for those that basically raised themselves from a small age, intimacy with people that they love can be extremely challenging. They fear rejection; they fear abandonment; and they fear being hurt like they were for years as a child. If they have not dealt with those, what I call, "intimacy issues", it will be nearly impossible for them to have a trusting, respectful, honest, and close personal relationship with anyone, let alone a beloved partner. Don't get me wrong, we all have some type of intimacy issues, right?

Now, if you add sexual abuse and/or repeated and negatively charged sexual experiences when growing up, then you have an even larger issue, which directly impacts the sexuality of in an intimate partnership. For these individuals, I have noticed that the more vulnerable and deeper the relationship, the more and more difficult it is to be physically intimate with that one you love. Think about it... it is easier for them to have sex with people who do not matter than it is to have sex with you, who does. You represent love, which terrifies them because they believe you will leave them, hurt them, and, ultimately, abandon them. It is all in avoidance of pain. I'm not gonna lie – it really stinks. This is so common nowadays and we all need to remind ourselves to have a great amount of compassion for people in similar situations. But, they can seek help! And, though it is not easy and it could take several years of hard work, the freedom and the rewards of physical intimacy done well will be worth every penny, literally.

Paolo and I were seeing a counselor, mostly to work on his/our intimacy issues. I was in a quandary because it was the first time in a long while that I felt I was going to build my life and a family with my boyfriend.

At the most challenging times of our two-year relationship, I was traveling pretty much every other ten to twelve days to Mexico, so there was ample time for Paolo to get lonely, horny, and find boys. Even though we had agreed to be monogamous, he was evidently out having *hot* sex with other guys.

We had been having quite the dry spell (that refers to our sex life, in case you were confused). We continued to go to therapy like good little doobies, but we were still not being all that physically intimate. This in itself was trying on both of us, as he really wanted to, but just couldn't... and I really wanted to, but was sometimes too caught up in my insecurities due to the lack of sex. Again, since he had quite a heavy childhood with unfortunate events all over the place, as much as Paolo wanted to be able to make love to me, his physical intimacy issues were just too much. Sigh!

Throughout most of July, he continued to be sick, have fevers, diarrhea, colds, etc... and he could not seem to break free from whatever was ailing his body. On Monday, the 3rd of August, we went to the doctor's office together. We both thought it would be prudent to confirm his negative status for the slew of sexually transmitted diseases, and of course take the always-fun HIV test. I had just been tested at the end of May, so we felt it was not necessary for me to get tested.

For some reason, both Paolo and our doctor were pretty concerned that an HIV-related issue could be causing his symptoms. I, of course, was in complete denial of this. I mean, we had only done one three-way over the past 2-3 months... and I knew I had never cheated on him — as much as I may have wanted to — so I was beyond perplexed. I was spending a lot of money to have a Licensed Clinical Social Worker help him to be more intimate with me. You might say I was in complete and utter denial that he would cheat on me...or just plan naïve.

Once he had taken his tests, Paolo was *convinced* that he was HIV+. He went so far as to say that he would commit suicide if he found out that he was HIV+. I knew that was just his sexy, dark and dramatic humor, but I also sensed that there was some truth to it. He was pretty depressed for the next couple of days.

My job at the time was Director of Resource Planning for a company that grows lemons, meaning I was in charge of H.R., payroll, daily operations, the security and maintenance of all buildings, facilities, and the ranches where we actually grew the lemons. I don't want to brag, but I was kind of a bigwig down there.

On Wednesday of that particular week, it was time for me to fly to Mexico. The results were supposed to be in on Thursday or Friday. I had always learned to put any worry aside while waiting for HIV test results because otherwise it would drive me insane. I honestly was *not* worried at all.

Boy, I definitely should have been.

Getting to Mexico was no easy task. It was usually a four-hour plane ride, then a one-hour plane ride, followed by a four to six-hour car ride (or longer, depending on certain traffic conditions such as military stops, road closures, transportation strikes, cartel barricades, etc.) On this particular day, of that particular week, we made amazing time.

It was like clockwork. The moment I put my stuff down, I received a call from my boyfriend. Due to Paolo's foreign accent, it was already a bit challenging to understand what he was saying, let alone, when he was crying, and I had never, *ever* heard him cry until that day. I could not understand what he was saying. He said... in his cute little accent, "The doctor called and I have

HIV." I was like… what??? I was hoping for one small second that our Mexico-L.A. cell phone to cell phone lines had crossed with someone else's. Paolo repeated his statement and my heart melted.

My first thought was about him and how his life was going to change. My second thought was that I had to leave and return home after making a 24-hour journey to arrive. My third and fourth thoughts were that I had to find my boss, let him know what was going on, and then have one of the security guards drive me back to the airport. My fifth thought was that it would be extremely difficult to fly out of Mexico City at night… the last plane left at around 8:30 pm and it was already 1 pm, and it would take four hours at least to return to the airport. My sixth thought was about my job and how disappointed I was that all my business decisions were going to have to wait for another two weeks. Notice that none of these thoughts were about my safety. And all of those thoughts happened in probably ten seconds.

My next sentiment was that of **Shock** and disbelief. I asked if the results could be a false positive. Somehow, through his broken tears and broken heart, he explained to me that for the type of test that he took, there was no such thing as a false positive. That specific test searched for a number of antibodies, and apparently his result was off the charts. It was beyond confirmed. Me, and my stupid self, continuing in my **Shock** and denial, was insistent that he get tested again. Paolo demanded that I speak to the doctor right away and come home right away. I said, "Of course. I'm on it. Where are you?" "I am on the floor…" was his reply. I said, "Don't move! I will call you back as soon as I can. We will get through this, no matter what. I'm not going to leave you… I will

stay and we will get through this. I love you. I'll call you back."
That was me… always the upbeat one… always the one to know
exactly what to say in almost every situation. I really meant those
words to him… given everything we had been through, I really
meant those words.

I called the doctor. Obviously, he could not explain anything to
me without my Paolo's permission. Therefore, he had to contact
my boyfriend, and then contact me. In the interim I called my
travel agent and had her start looking for flights. After about ten
minutes, I was speaking with the doctor. He confirmed Paolo's
HIV positive status. After a long pause on my end, he said, "Seth,
you need to come in and get tested right away." …Um… hello?
That was the first time it occurred to me that I might be positive
as well. It was terrifying. I almost dropped the phone. It hit me
like a ton of bricks. Oh my God, I could have it! He could have
given me HIV. I know I did not cheat… so it must have been the
three-way…

After our in-depth conversation about the next steps, I hung up
the phone, took three deep breaths, almost fainted, but then composed myself. I knew in this instance, there was no room for
Shock, no room for denial, and no room for anything but dealing
with this head-on and right now. God was I scared.

I immediately called his best friend in L.A., and in the most desperate voice I said, "I need you… I need you to go sit with him
until I get home. Hopefully, I can get back tonight." He asked me
what was going on… all I could say was, "Paolo just tested positive for HIV!!!" His friend took a deep breath in… and said, "I'm
on my way!" It was the first moment that any emotion grabbed
me. That's a true friend, man. (To be honest, I still get teary-eyed

when I think about that moment. Thanks for being there that day. You know who you are!)

I called my Paolo back. He asked, "Did you speak to the doctor?"... Sniffle, sniffle.

"Yes! I told you before and I'm telling you again, we will get through this. I love you. I adore you and no matter what, we will get through this together!"

"Are you coming home?"

"Yes, I just need to speak with my boss. I hope I can get home tonight. I will let you know. Your best friend is on his way over to you right now. I called him and he will stay with you until I get there!"

"O...(sniffle)...kay...(sniffle). Is it for sure that I have HIV?"

"It looks like it."

I went on to tell him the plan. He started crying again when he realized he might have passed it on to me. (God that must feel awful!) When we hung up, I felt a tremendous amount of weight on my back, my shoulders, and everywhere in my body, essentially. I know this is crazy, but for the next eleven hours until I got to him, I could not think of anything other than that he just cannot have it. It was **Shock** to the nth degree.

I had to tell my boss. He was out driving around the ranch, as he often did, in his VIP pick-up truck. It was absolutely beautiful there, filled with hundreds of acres of lemon trees. The roads were normally empty, with the sweet smell of lemons piercing intensely through the air. There were miles and miles of lemon trees everywhere. It was incredible – breathtaking!

My boss and I were very close and he knew Paolo pretty well. He immediately picked me up and took me for a joy ride… which was probably about fifteen minutes, but felt like two hours. I could tell you exactly the route he took to get around. I could tell you every bump, if you want. All of my senses were heightened during that ride. I could think of nothing other than getting the hell out of there, getting my butt on a plane and embracing Paolo.

My boss was silent for a bit before he said to me, "I guess you guys aren't as monogamous as you thought." At the time, I thought he was quite insensitive to say something like that, but in retrospect, he really wanted to protect my behind, literally and figuratively. His main focus was *me*. And, it was clear to him that my main focus should have been me too! He was overly generous and extremely understanding.

By some God-given miracle, I made a 6:30 pm flight to Mexico City and then had thirty-five minutes to make the next flight. I ran like hell. I made it, and I even had time to buy a stuffed animal to bring home to my boyfriend.

At the gate they gave me some trouble about my Aadvantage Gold status… and they were not going to let me on the plane! I handled it like a pro. I told them that there was an emergency at home, and that I needed to be on that plane more than I had ever needed to be on a plane before. (What? I never said I wasn't dramatic.) When I sat down in my seat, dripping with sweat, I thanked God for letting me get home.

The very next moment, the idea for this book was born. It was on that flight home. It was on that amazingly *long* flight home.

We landed at 11:59 pm and my boyfriend and his best friend were there to pick me up. It felt like I had just swum across the Amazon in piranha and caiman-infested waters to get home. He was a wreck. I was a wreck... and so was his best friend.

In this instance of **Shock**, I have to say that every minute felt like an eternity. I would say I was a bit of a zombie, but I was a zombie with passion and a purpose. I was so focused on getting home and comforting him that I did exactly what I had to do. Even when I am in **Shock**, I get very clear about the facts very quickly. I knew that I was not going to leave him. I knew that this would definitely complicate our sex lives and intimacy even more. I knew that he would be beside himself with emotion. I guess I knew too that our lives would never be the same.

Amidst all of these things that I knew, and all of the literal **Shock** waves going through my mind, I really hoped that it was a bad dream and that at some point I would wake up drenched in sweat. Alas, that never happened... and the reality of the situation became more and more real over the next few days. You can be in **Shock** all you want, but that does not mean it is not really happening to you. Trust me, I know.

To Be Continued...

Un Secuestro en México – A Kidnapping in Mexico

I know. I know. It's a weird subtitle. I am going to give you a good briefing of exactly what happened to me, that terrible day, in Mexico. It was August of 2010. It was beyond HOT! It was a regular morning on a regular Wednesday. I was stoked because I was leaving the next day to go home. The last day was always charged with enthusiasm, a shit-ton of work, lots of questions, lots of meetings, but it always seemed doable because I was pretty much on my way home.

Originally, when I started this position as the Director of Resource Planning, I knew that Mexico was in an unofficial internal war, but I had *no* idea just how bad it was. But the job was incredible – literally amazing! I pretty much turned a blind eye to the violence and murders happening daily. At about the fourteen-month mark, things started to get extremely dangerous in our little area of Mexico. It continues to be a very coveted part of the country that still does not have a settled cartel leader; so three cartels have been vying for the area, as well as the military and the Special Ops teams we would see from time to time. And, yes, it is a war.

There were two locations to and from which we traveled on a daily basis and they were about ninety kilometers away from one another. It was pretty typical to be stopped at least once or twice per trip by some type of security detail or police checkpoint. And since we had a beast of a Suburban and it was armored, we were consistently stopped and searched. That wasn't the scary part.

I would always have to make the choice of whether to speak in Spanish or in English only. I do speak fluent Spanish, but sometimes for my safety, it was better that I kept my mouth shut, so they could not ask me questions because there could be trouble otherwise. Sometimes, I couldn't resist speaking in Spanish.

That morning we were making good time. Everything in my life seemed great. Suddenly, we were pulled over in the middle of a major cross-section of four roads. I thought it was a bit of an odd place to pull us over. They were local police, or so I thought...

In Mexico, there are three types of police: the Local Police (most corrupt), the Staties (a little less corrupt), and the National Police (the least corrupt of them all... especially since they patrol the same areas as the military). So, this time, it was the local police... and I got a little scared as we had *never* been pulled over by local police.

Once they had ascertained that there was more than just the driver in the vehicle, they asked us to pull over to the side of the road. By us, I mean my Executive Protection Agent (my body-guard) and myself.

Within fifteen seconds, this huge, what appeared to be "Police Van" pulled in front of the Suburban, so that it literally hid the entirety of our vehicle from anyone's sight. This was my first clue that something was wrong. Only two people got out of the "Police Van". They asked us to step outside our vehicle. Within forty-five more seconds, a "local" police car with four "police" arrived, and they immediately got out their machine guns and pointed them at us. There were now six machine guns pointed at the two of us. Again, this was NOT routine. After we gave them our passports and identification, they seemed bothered that I was American. Bothered in the way that I was definitely going to put a hole in their plans.

They asked us a slew of questions and YES I spoke Spanish for this one, folks. I knew there was something awry. They would NOT let us move. It was a bit like... uh... where are my American rights? Yeah, right. In Mexico, you are in Mexico, end of story. Being American is only going to provoke them more. Having more *cojones* than most, I inquired about the hold up. They finally told us, after some silence, that we were waiting for their "boss" who apparently was the chief of police. So we waited for him. Another two minutes passed and this white Jetta arrived on the scene, with tires screeching and throwing dust/sand everywhere. He was clearly the boss of these guerrillas.

As he was walking up to us, I caught a glimpse of two things: 1) there was no police equipment in the "Po-Po Van" - it was completely empty and 2) there was a lady in the car of the plump "bossman". When he walked up to us - don't forget six machine guns were still being pointing at us - he was giving me the dirtiest look imaginable. I immediately noticed that he had two cell phones... one pink and the other more of a smartphone. Everyone knows that in Mexico, *no one* has two phones unless you are a cartel member. I knew that because a new law had recently passed in Mexico, that even for pay-as-you-go phones, phones needed to be registered with your social security-type number. So, I thought, aha! You are not police. Of course, I could not say that... but my guard was on high alert. Of course, I had no idea how I was going to get out of this situation with my vehicle. I knew they wanted the armored vehicle.

Bossman was fat, rather ugly, and had a really bitchy flair about him. They all acted as if I had blotched their plans. We spent thirty minutes there with Bossman while he asked question after question. He asked me the more routine questions, of course, but he also asked me a bunch of questions that were, in my opinion, outside of the regular "security" or "police" questions. Then they ransacked the inside of our vehicle. This was yet another indication to me that they were *not* police. Anybody working for the military or the like would always put things back into place - these guys left everything torn and ripped apart. He even went so far as to ask me to open my laptop and explain to him what I had on there.

The Mexican cartels go around terrorizing both the Mexican people and the government. The threat of being carjacked or kidnapped never subsides. Each cartel has its own special technique for how to terrorize. I became convinced that my persecutors were members of the Zetas, who are amongst the most deadly of cartels.

While this fatso "distracted" me in real time, someone at a computer (who kept calling the Bossman on the pink phone) was researching us. They soon knew the name of the company we worked for. They soon had enough pieces of information to figure out that my company was owned by friends of the Clintons. To be honest, I really think that ticked them off the most. They were there for the awesome armored Suburban and were deterred by my being an American who had connections with the Clintons. No one wants to piss off the Clintons... even in Mexico, they know their reach.

I was pretty upset and irritated by this whole process and was trying to be as nice as possible, but I could not help throwing out some snide comments. Finally, after forty-five minutes or so, I had had enough. I mean, if you are going to take the car, take the damn car already! Right? I picked up my phone that was thrown on the floor. The machine gun-toting 25-year-old to my left, who did not like my snide comments at all, pointed his gun right at me. I continued to pick up my phone… and I started to look for Lieutenant Enriquez' number.

A few months prior, we had made friends with a military officer in our region who told us that if we ever got stopped or felt uncomfortable, we should call him right away, and he would send troops within minutes. They would frequent our properties, checking the grounds for possible criminals and cartels, and in exchange, we would give them cold Cokes and bottled waters. Pretty good deal, I thought! I honestly never thought I would need his help… until this moment.

Bossman demanded to know what I was doing. I replied that I was calling my friend Lieutenant Enriquez. I used that man's name to the fullest extent I could - I spoke loudly and clearly, "Lieutenant *ENRIQUEZ!*" Bossman looked stunned and asked how I knew that man. I casually relayed to him that the Lieutenant was a friend to my company and had advised me to call him if I ever felt uncomfortable at a "checkpoint" or "stop-point". Boy, did Bossman give me the stare-down of my life. He got on the pink phone and left the immediate area. He was obviously speaking to *his* boss. He came back, giving me another dirty look. Then, by some miracle, he simply nodded his head and let us go. I was **Shock**ed. I was even more impressed that I did not pee my pants.

Within seconds, all of the cars were gone! (We were left to clean up the ransacked vehicle.) My first call was to my boss. The smart man that he was, he definitely did not want me to panic, so he intimated that it seemed pretty routine to him. He knew just as well as my security guard and I knew that we had just managed to save the vehicle and ourselves from being carjacked or kidnapped.

By this time, we had made it to the second location safely, and I ran into the bathroom, so as to not burst into tears in front of my team. That would have made me look weak, and I definitely did not want that. I remember sitting on the toilet saying, "Oh, My God… I think I was just almost kidnapped. God. OMG. What the hell just happened?!"

My second call was to my boyfriend who had *no* idea what to say to me. At the beginning he was not the most supportive… I'm sure this just threw him for a loop.

More than 47,500 people have died in drug-related violence in Mexico since December 2006, when Calderon took office and announced plans to deploy troops to combat cartels[4]. Two weeks before this last trip down to Mexico, five human heads were found about seven kilometers from where I lay my head down to sleep at night. Yes, human heads. I went down there month after month, because, after all, it was my job. Ironically, I was in charge of security.

That day I completed a very detailed report about the occurrence, did everything I had to do, met with everyone I needed to meet with… I imagine I was pretty much a walking zombie. I felt like my mind had completely frozen and my body was just doing everything it could to keep going.

---

4   "Mexico's Calderon Defends Drug War in Final State of Nation Address," CNN. com, September 4, 2012.

I was amazed that I had an insatiable appetite that day and night. I realized that when major life experiences happen, I take pleasure in eating comfort food and junk food. I eat very healthily all the time, except for the occasional chocolate dessert. But when I am in **Shock** or overwhelmed by emotions, I do not hesitate to eat tons of pizza, burgers, fries, Cool Ranch Doritos and Pepsi. I usually have a soft drink about once a month or less, so for me it is a huge deal. I ate everything I could find… Coke, Doritos, Chiflets (salted dried bananas), etc. I just could not eat enough. I didn't do any work when I got home… I watched three or four movies in a row, all in an effort to forget what had just happened.

That night I could not get to sleep. I was sooooo excited to leave that god-awful area, not to mention the terrifying country of Mexico. I have never been back since.

I was convinced that God was looking out for me that day (and I am not a religious man, rather, a spiritual one).

This time I was in **Shock** until I made it home to the U.S.A. Once home, I finally cried. I actually kissed the DFW airport's ground when I landed on American soil. As I have mentioned previously, even when in **Shock**, there is a part of my mind that takes over to get done what needs to be done. It is an incredible unconscious response which allows me to continue to function at a highly efficient level, while the world falls apart beside me. I must admit that I am a bit obsessive-compulsive about certain things. When the **Shock** sets in, my O.C.D. and logistics brain actually comes in handy as it takes over immediately, and I do not miss a beat.

To Be Continued…

The Day Manhattan Stood Still

The Day The Earth Stood Still. This was the day that war and hate came crashing down on the United States of America. This day did not just impact the United States, but the entire world. I was living in New York City at the time. I thought I had experienced everything; from being held up at knifepoint, to movie premieres at the Ziegfeld, from the amazing Bronx Zoo, to drunken trannies. Boy, was I mistaken.

I was making my way to work. I was working in the garment industry as a production assistant, and had to travel frequently to the sweatshops in Chinatown. Just kidding, they weren't sweatshops, but I used to joke with all of my friends that they were. I mean, there were definitely 200-300 persons working hard, crunched and sweating profusely in non-air-conditioned factories in old Manhattan Chinatown buildings. It looked like a sweatshop to me, but there was no child labor, or at least not in the front rooms! It was a Tuesday morning. I do not remember anything up until 8:48am.

I arrived at the production office and my boss informed me that a small plane had hit one of the towers of the World Trade Center. Probably like most New Yorkers, I thought it was a private plane giving a tour that got too close, but I was intrigued. After chatting for approximately twenty minutes, she gave me my instructions for the day: to help support the "sweatshops" and make sure some big shipment was sent out that day. I was about to leave when my boss told me that all of the subways were closed, so I would have to take a bus down to Canal Street. I went to the subway to see for myself. There were police in the station and the trains were stopped. Okay, it was true. I got on the bus, which was completely packed due to the closure of the subway.

We got to 34th and Broadway, and the bus driver announced that all public transportation had been ordered to stop because a second plane had just hit the second tower. "I have to let you off, folks. The City of New York is shutting down all public transportation and bridges." This caused quite the uproar on the bus. My first thought was, "Oh, my God! If they are closing down all public transportation and closing all of the bridges, how are people going to get back to Brooklyn and Queens? And am I glad I don't live there…"

At around 9:10 am, I got off the bus and walked back to the office eight blocks away. When I arrived, I told them we might be under attack in a completely surreal and serene, non-dramatic state, and that I was going home. We definitely were not going to get that shipment out today… and I was positive that the huge client in Texas would understand. Stunned, I proceeded to walk home. It was only about two miles, which ordinarily took me about thirty minutes. This day, it took me about sixty, arriving home at 10:10am, twelve minutes after the first tower had fallen. There were so many sirens, people running in all directions - utter chaos. The usual New Yorker pace was slowed down to a crawl of disappointment, sadness, and complete **Shock**. And, on every street corner, looking South, you could not only see the mobs of people walking North, but you could also see both towers smoking. It was beyond horrible; it was dumbfounding.

On that "long walk home", I had NEVER seen so many people in my life. I lived on 54th and 2nd, near the 59th Street Bridge which everybody had to cross in order to get to Queens, Sunnyside, Astoria, etc., and it was one of the only bridges that was open. As I got closer to home, people started to look more and more like zombies walking than people. I entered my apartment in a trance.

I missed seeing the first tower collapse live, as you know. But I did watch from my living room the second tower crumble at 10:28am. I could not believe what I was seeing. I could not fathom the thought of New York City without the Trade Towers. I just could not process this information quickly enough.

It was about at that time that I heard from my family. I remember all cell phones were down, yet miraculously my sister got through to me. She was so relieved. I told her to tell my family that I was okay. It definitely was not like today when one could just post on Facebook, "I'm alive!" and everyone would know. She is always the first one to call when there is a huge emergency going on, and it may seem to her that I usually happen to be living where the terrorists strike, the kidnappers strike, or the earthquakes strike. Jeez.

For the rest of the day, I watched the hoards of zombies walking up the street from my windows. After about 12 pm, I noticed that the people walking outside were covered in what looked like a gray ash. It took me a few minutes to realize that it was soot from the collapsed buildings. It was incredible, awe-striking, and haunting. Mostly it was just plain sad. Everyone was in complete **Shock** and was just going through the motions of getting home. All they cared about was getting home to their family and loved ones. Everyone was glued to the TV… or, at least, I was, for three days straight.

Have you heard about the BoatLift? It was the largest sea evacuation in history[5]. In World War II, 339,000 British and French soldiers were evacuated (sea-lifted) from Dunkirk over the course of nine days. On 9/11, nearly 500,000 civilians were sea-lifted from Lower Manhattan in just shy of nine hours. It brings tears to my eyes even as I write this. There is a powerful little twelve-minute documentary, narrated by Tom Hanks, about this incredible BoatLift. Check it out!

During those three days, I did not sleep or eat much. That is usually what happens to me when I am in **SHOCK**. My whole body slows down and I, myself, become a zombie. I barely spoke to my partner at that time. Don't get me wrong, I was thrilled that he was at home, alive, and did not have any nightmare stories about that particular day. I mean, I have friends that were caught underground for hours with no electricity. My experience was not as severe as others. I have other friends who actually abandoned the Towers. My own boyfriend was due to go into the World Trade Center that very morning, but for some reason, was running thirty minutes late, thank God! That unusual tardiness most likely not only saved his life, but also saved him from an absolutely horrific first-hand experience of running down eighty flights of stairs and being covered in gray soot.

I lived in NYC for five more years, prior to moving to LA. I can tell you that New Yorkers do not speak about 9/11. It hardly ever comes up and we also do not refer to the World Trade Center as Ground Zero, either. Whenever out-of-towners came and stayed

---

5   BoatLift, An Untold Story of 9/11 Resilience - http://www.youtube.com/watch?v=XbTRL7B3g38, http://www.oprah.com/blogs/Hope-Floats-The-Boatlift-of-911

with me, they would always want to visit "Ground Zero". My response was always the same: we can go see it, only if you refer to it as the World Trade Center or the Twin Towers.

Two years after 9/11, I remembered something important. Here it goes… when I looked at my watch the morning of September 11th, it read 8:48am. I was at 42nd and 6th Avenue. Out of nowhere, I heard this very loud noise above. I remember looking up, along with everybody else around me. This noise kept getting louder and louder and closer and closer. All of a sudden, I saw this large commercial airplane fly right above my head. It was flying at about the altitude of the top of the Empire State Building and I said to myself, I really hope it doesn't hit anything. Do you know that even when the Twin Towers came down, I still did not put two and two together? Nope, it appears that a part of me was in **Shock** for two years. It actually took me two years to remember that I saw the plane that crashed into the first Tower with my own eyes.

There is another thing that I remember about the W.T.Cs. Every Thursday night at the top of one of the towers, there was a Swing event (not couple's swinging, my perverted friends, I mean swing dancing). I had been at the top of the towers the Thursday prior, looking out from the top of the world, and thinking how magnifi-cent the view was… and what an amazing *feat* these towers were, and what a symbol of power they were for the whole world. And then five days later, they were no longer.

To Be Continued…

A Friend Taken Too Young

Let's face it: losing a friend just sucks. From beginning to end, the process is exhausting, sad, and just plain hard. The feelings and emotions associated are in constant flux and constant disarray. These things are just not supposed to happen to us, right? In my particular life, I lost my best friend Luli when she was twenty-six. Way too young. The date: March 13th. The year: 2003. That's when this world lost one of the good ones.

This was just before the time of Facebook and Myspace, so I found out about Luli's passing through a group email. Can you believe it? A group email? It was from a distant mutual friend of ours, Ochhi, saying something like, "I can't believe it... my heart goes out to Majo and her family". I was like... what? Majo, short for María José, is Luli's sister and one of my truest soul mates in this world. I immediately emailed my questions to Occhi, and she emailed me right back replying that Luli had passed away.

I don't think we are ever quite prepared to handle the deaths of close friends, especially without warning. It feels weird, unnatural, and devastating. When I received her emailed response, I collapsed into the back of my chair, took a deep inhale, and even longer exhale. I could not believe my eyes. A tiny part of me was clinging to the possibility that it wasn't true. I just couldn't believe it. I couldn't believe that my friend, Luli, was gone. I would never see her again. Gross!

I was at work, but I dialed Ochhi's international number and spoke directly to her for about fifteen minutes, asking for more details. Sadly, she did not have a great amount of information. Once I hung up the phone, I took another inhale and exhale and just looked out my Manhattan office window at the construction going on outside. Now I had confirmation that it was, in fact, true, yet I still could not fathom what I had just learned. Really? Can it be real? Is she dead? What on earth happened?

I was in complete **Shock**. Next thing I knew, I ran into my boss' office and advised her that I would be leaving for the day, as I had just found out that one of my best friends had passed away... and I would probably need to fly to Ecuador for the next couple of days, but I would let her know the plan. Looking back, it was a bit dramatic, but, gimme a break, I was only twenty-four years old. She was my first super close friend to pass away. I lost an amazing friend that day and I almost could not wrap my head around it.

I had previously planned to visit my grandparents in New Haven that weekend. My grandparents were aging and we always had so much fun there together, but this death was of great importance to me too. I frantically looked for flights as if my life depended on it. I called every airline and looked on every online site, to little avail.

All the time while looking for flights, all the time while dreading that call to Majo, I still just could not believe that she was gone. It was really too much for me to handle. It was crazy. How could this have happened? And she was so young. How is that fair? What the hell happened? I still didn't have any details or any specifics.

Hours after being home, I finally had built up enough courage to call Luli's family. It was a relief to speak to Majo. My first words were "I'm coming… when do I need to be there?" She was unbelievably composed and monotone in her reply. She advised that the burial would be at 12pm the following day, directly follow by the religious funeral services from 2-4pm. That gave me approximately sixteen hours to get to Quito, Ecuador. Ugh. I knew the chances were slim. Her tone was soft and eerily calm. No doubt in **Shock**, Majo was articulate and poised throughout our five-minute conversation.

I wanted to offer condolences, offer her all of my thoughts and prayers, and my strength. After all, she had just lost her only sister, who was her best friend in life. I had so many questions and so many emotions, but I felt it was simply the wrong time to request details. Our conversation was all about logistics. I told her that flights were $1300 that night… and it was so expensive, but I would see what I could do. I was determined. I was frantic, and I was panicking. I had just paid off a great deal of my debts. I really did *not* want to incur more debt, but this was *Luli's funeral*.

Even after speaking with Majo, it was hard to believe that Luli was gone. I was speechless. It was a little hard to breathe and this was happening whether I wanted it to or not. Her passing was out of my control. She was just too young and it was very very unfair. I felt a huge emptiness within me and I felt such helplessness. I needed to travel to Ecuador within sixteen hours from New York, and I had no idea how that was going to happen.

To Be Continued…

5 THINGS TO REMEMBER WHEN IN SHOCK

1.   Take Some Time Off!

Go Home. Don't work for a few days. Whatever you tell your co-workers, at least make sure you are honest and a little bit dramatic, or tell them your business is your business, right? In any case, take some time to adjust, relax, and re-group. It just might be all you need.

2.   Everything Will Be All Right.

Keep telling yourself it will all be okay. Shift your feelings. As the **Shock** *subsides, imagine the eventual outcome of what you desire most... the details or the "how" doesn't matter. Focus on the feeling and emotions you will feel upon having your desired outcome. Didn't work? Do it again. It takes a couple tries. This is a very strong and powerful technique, and I guarantee it works.*

3.   You Don't Have to Feel Anything!

It's absolutely okay not to be feeling anything. Nothing. Nothing at all. If it has been a few days, and you are still not feeling anything, that's okay, too. The truth will sink in. The truth might just be hard to deal with all at once. There is no rush.

4.   Moments of Extreme Clarity Will Happen!

The great thing here is that through these situations, clarity can smack you in the tukhus within the blink of an eye. Sometimes, the one thing you are avoiding and have been avoiding is the one exact thing you need to be doing. Be patient. Still feel nothing? Don't worry, you will!

5.   *There's Nothing to Worry About, Until There's Something to Worry About.*

Words to live by. Within our minds, we have the capacity to create monumental issues and anxiety over the tiniest of things or over issues that have not yet been confirmed. Do yourself a favor and do your best to worry only when there is something grave to worry about.

SHOCK - In Conclusion:

Whoa! - **Shock** is a natural, physical and emotional reaction to surprising and upsetting experiences, which are just too much for the human inside of us to handle at that very moment in time. It is that simple. It could be just too much. We are very complex beings, us humans. How amazing to know that the mind, body, and soul have instinctual and protective behaviors that are automatic and incredibly powerful! I am still in awe of this.

Shock is the body's way of saying, "**Whoa!** Hold up! What just happened?" or "What did you just say to me?" or just plain "What???" **Shock** is the necessary pause we need in order to handle whatever situation has presented itself. It is the delicious moment where reality and complete numbness meet. It is where the sleeping dogs lose sight of the fact that they are sleeping. It is an instinctual and reactionary response. It is a hollow emptiness, a timeless division, devoid of regular recognition. For some, it could last minutes... for others it could probably last years, on some level. We all have been through **Shock** and experienced it. We all will go through it again. You can't plan on anything in this world. Soon, in the very near future, we might not even be certain of death and taxes anymore!

This brings me to my next point... not missing a beat. We truly come alive and present during **Shock**. You may have noticed that this has been a recurring theme in all of my personal stories. When I go into **Shock**, I become uber-aware of everything that is going on around me. I notice that my emotions are more raw. I notice that the world seems much bigger and much more unknown to me. I become more present. It feels like I just finished a yoga class, and time has slowed down to almost a halt. Every moment is filled with something. Every moment is either filled with emotion or filled with action. I tell you this because knowledge is power.

In order to Smile From The Inside, I believe we all need to be aware of our coping and dealing process. To that end, I believe that we experience some sort of **Shock** first. Look, I'm leveling with you… everyone's coping and healing methods are just as unique as his or her original personality, but there are common threads and that is why I am writing this book. As you can see, even from my own examples, one's own process for various experiences can vary, or one can spend more time in one step/phase than another. I feel strongly that if people had a bit more knowledge and awareness of their own "grieving" or, rather, "**healing**" process, they would be more empowered to accept the situation at hand for what it is and move on that much faster.

The better aware you are of your own patterns of behavior, the better you can allow the situation to take its natural course and the less inclined you will be to judge yourself or beat yourself up. Sad things will happen. All we can do is increase the awareness of our process, honor our feelings, and let all that judgment go. Be good to yourself. You *will* deal with it. I promise, all this stuff will help you out in the end.

If you work to comprehend and overcome the **Shock**, you will have begun the Smile From The Inside process. It is not easy. No, it definitely is not easy. It *is* well worth the journey. Just like in yoga or any group fitness class, **Shock** is similar to warming up the body by doing the basics of moving through breath work or the basic principles for abdominal/core work.

Whenever you feel in **Shock**, check in with the above list for the 5 Things To Remember When in **Shock**. It will make things easier on you. That is what they are there for! HELP!!!

Shock prepares the mind and body for the extreme. It is the first important step we all must take to live a more authentic, more content, and more solid presence on this Earth. And that's what Smiling From The Inside is all about.

MOCK-CCEPTANCE

STAGE TWO: MOCK-CCEPTANCE.

Denial

noun

1. Refusal to acknowledge an unacceptable truth or emotion or to admit it into consciousness, used as a defense mechanism: *I was an addict in denial*[6].

2. In Psychoanalysis, a defense mechanism involving a disavowal or failure consciously to acknowledge thoughts, feelings, desires, or aspects of reality that would be painful or unacceptable, as

---

6   "Denial," Oxford Dictionary, 2012.

when a person with a terminal illness refuses to acknowledge the imminence of death[7].

3. One of the defense mechanisms that may be employed by individuals in dealing with stress or risk. In denial, a person unconsciously ignores or reinterprets anything that induces high stress or threatens the individual's feeling of security. By paying attention to only certain parts of a situation or event, the person protects her or himself from other parts that are frightening[8].

Expressed Feeling = "I'm fine!"

Part-Denial, Part-Acceptance. It's **Mock-cceptance.**

Mock-cceptance to me is denial and *fake* acceptance all wrapped into one. Above is how the experts define denial. The last definition is the most closely aligned with my own personal definition. Even when in denial, there are moments of truth and reality that sneak their way in. After **Shock**, there comes a re-understanding of the current circumstances - what I like to call **Mock-cceptance.** I like to think about it as a denied acceptance.

In the phrase, "**I'm Fine**," there comes a false and re-assuring acceptance, which allows you to believe that you are feeling good, perhaps even great. In actuality you are still dealing with the event that has just occurred. Sometimes you even feel on top of the world. Denial is bliss. I know, I know. It has been said

---

7   Colman, Andrew M, Oxford Dictionary of Psychology. Oxford University Press, 2009.

8   Beins, Bernard, Feldman, Alan J., and Gall, Susan, *The Gale Encyclopedia of Psychology*, Gale, 1996.

before, but listen to this: if you think about it, denial is the most amazing emotional coping mechanism EVER! It is natural and fat-free... what a bonus! I believe it is the mind and heart's way of *gently* breaking you into the reality of the situation at hand. It is another natural and instinctual response, which allows you the chance to wrap your head around the idea. Denial really is a blessing. Enjoy it.

I do believe that there is an inherent truth in the acceptance at this point of the process that creeps inside and stirs quiet for a bit of time. I do feel it not only helps but it also actually prepares you for the rest of the healing journey. As we all know, it is not always a pleasant yellow-brick road, but it's *your* yellow-brick road! So enjoy the **Mock-cceptance** and know that it is imperative that you pass through this beautifully disguised covered bridge, if you will. Feel safe. You are safe.

If **Shock** is preparing the mind and body for what's next, then **Mock-cceptance**, as you will come to understand, is where the autopilot takes over as the juices start flowing, and all seems to be good and right. Acknowledgement of **Mock-cceptance** will bring you one step closer to the Smile From The Inside way of being. Through the following continuation of my personal stories, you will learn how **Mock-cceptance** is the next necessary stage in the S.M.I.L.E. Method for healing.

Um... You Lost Me At Cancer

Cancer is never an easy subject. I do hope that as time progresses, cancer will become a threat that we can surmount with medicine and technology. It already has a bit, but we're still not there yet. By the time I learned I had cancer, I knew it did not necessarily mean a death sentence, even though our minds and emotions might go there within the blink of an eye. Just because you get cancer does *not* mean you will receive radiation, or support chemo, let alone die. It would have been nice if someone had been continuously reassuring me of that fact. Words to the wise!

And now, back to my story. After meeting with the oncologist, my new "buzz word" at the time, I just could not go back to work that Wednesday afternoon. I would have to wait TWO MORE days to find out my fate... to find out the stage of cancer and to find out just how much my life would change. Would I lose my hair? Would I lose body parts? Would I need radiation? Or worse... chemo? You cannot even imagine what was going through my mind. Upon leaving the John Wayne Cancer Institute in Santa Monica, I started driving home without even thinking. You know when you are just driving and then figuratively wake up moments later thinking to yourself, oh, my God, where did I just go? You mean I've been driving this whole time? It was one of those drives. I was not upset, sad, or beyond myself. I think I was emotion-less, which, if you knew me (which you are starting to do) you would know that that does not happen very often. It takes an incredible event to put me into that state. Again, I am human and this is a perfectly natural human response.

Just to back-up for a second... when I told my parents and closest friends earlier that week that I had cancer, I seemed remarkably together... and I could not figure out for the life of me why. I could not figure out how I could keep my composure, go to work, be productive, have conversations with people, etc.... Now, of course, it all makes sense to me. I was completely in the **Mock-cceptance** stage of healing. For about two weeks, depending on the situation, I passed through this this stage of denied acceptance. This is where everything appears to be functioning at the status quo. It is where I feel as if everything will be A-okay, where the sun rises and sets like it always has, and even though I have cancer and am perfectly aware of that fact, I will be fine. It is definitely a deceiving phase of awareness. Again, don't be surprised if you feel good, or even excellent.

In my emotionless state, driving home from my very first oncologist appointment, (Yikes!) I drove past a Whole Foods and, all of a sudden, I got an incredible urge for a cookie. Do you know that Whole Foods used to have 4" round chocolate chip organic cookies, which were the absolute BEST in the world? I actually turned the car around, and found parking, which in that area was always a challenge! I clearly wanted that cookie and felt that I deserved anything that I wanted in those days.

The act of buying the chocolate chip cookie became a routine event and more of a reward to myself after every subsequent oncology visit... until they discontinued those big cookies. That was a very sad day. I searched all over for those darn cookies, only to learn from the bakers that they had been discontinued. It was quite emotional for me. Then it dawned on me that those cookies were one of my coping mechanisms throughout the entire cancer experience. It was completely a psychological blow for me that they were no longer available. The cookies are now horrible-tasting and small.

That first day, however, that cookie hit just the spot. Yummy. That was all I needed to feel satisfied. Not really, but that is what I told myself regardless. Now, I would need to keep myself busy for the next 48 hours or so. The TiVo just didn't have enough available shows and/or movies in the queue or on-demand, By some miraculous gift from God, I was able to sleep that night. Probably because I hadn't been able to sleep the previous two nights and I was emotionally and absolutely exhausted. Emotional exhaustion is so much more tiring than physical exhaustion.

I thought I would reach out to my ex at that point and tell him what was going on. He was beyond stunned and offered his support and love, which was really all that I wanted. After all, he had been by my side for the previous two years… and I thought I really needed him at the time. Probably not the best decision I could have made looking back, but I felt extremely alone and desperate. Little did I know, he was already dating someone else, a surprise to me!

The next morning I went to work. I had to. It probably sounds weird to most of you, but I had to do something with all of that time during the day. My co-workers planned on taking me out that night as well, so as to keep my mind occupied. I'll never forget, though, when one of my bosses, the less sensitive one, (who, I'm convinced, was always jealous of me, because I was younger and cuter) asked me, "What are you doing here, at the office?" I was stunned. I couldn't answer. He said, "If I were you, I would be home." My first thought was, "How insensitive!" My second thought was, "Wow," and after a long pause of about 10-15 seconds, I looked him straight in the eye and said, "I need to be here. I need something to do. Can you understand that?" I attempted to take my time to gracefully run to the bathroom with as much dignity as I could, and to fight back the tears. I barely made it into the stall before I started crying.

That's the funny thing about this stage of **Mock-cceptance**. There are moments when the reality starts to sink in, and for a couple minutes, you might feel an intense amount of emotion and pain. It's in those moments where the mind/body briefly allows you to see/glimpse just what you are up against in the healing months ahead. To be honest, I didn't particularly have much respect for the guy before that day, so it was easy for me to just have NO respect for him after this. Thinking about it with some reflection, perhaps he was trying to be supportive, but I definitely didn't receive it that way... not at all.

Vaguely, I remember the tasks for that insane week. I was doing expenses. I, for some reason, LOVE all things to do with numbers, expenses, budgets, reconciliations, etc. I think because the tasks and problems are finite and, in the end, always come out perfectly. Did I mention that those were some of the worst three days of my life, if not *the* worst? Now that I think about it, they were THE worst three days of my humble existence. I was so numb and raw. I won't keep you in suspense for too long about this. It's one of those times when it's too much to take it one day at a time, so you have to take it one moment at a time. That works too!

About 11 am on Friday, I got the call. It was my oncologist. I imagine he must dread those types of calls when he has bad news. In my case, however, he, from the get-go, sounded very optimistic. I remember going into the nearest office, which had no lights and was pretty much pitch black, and slammed the door behind me. I don't remember the details of the conversation at all. I'll tell you what I got from the conversation:

1) I needed to have surgery right away – the next Friday, in fact.

2) I needed to have a procedure called a lymph-node biopsy, which he had actually pioneered several years prior. In this procedure, they inject radioactive chemicals into the location nearest to the melanoma, and then do several x-rays over the course of 30 minutes to pinpoint which lymph nodes to remove. He thought that if the nearest lymph nodes were removed, there would be little to no chance that the cancer could spread.

3) He thought they would probably need to take out at least four to six lymph nodes. I said, "Oh, my God...that many???" He commented that we have about eight hundred of them. Oh, okay. Phew! I was relieved. Lol.

4) The cancer went beyond the marks of the original biopsy, so he didn't know how or if the cancer had spread. Ugh. That was not good news.

5) He was pretty confident that it was stage one, and he reiterated that it was an amazing blessing that we caught it this early, as it could have easily spread.

6) He would not know until after surgery whether or not I would need additional chemo/radiation. (God, I thought...we still don't know!)

7) He wanted to excise the area around my melanoma as early as possible, and that it would be an outpatient procedure, unless something went wrong.

He was definitely encouraging and reassuring while I asked him my, what felt like, fifty questions. The oncologist was extremely patient with me and understanding. Again, I wasn't really feeling much. In fact, I didn't really feel much at all until about two weeks after my surgery. Everyone in my office was super supportive, even the less sensitive ones. The next week was excruciatingly long as well, but I somehow managed to survive. My father and sister wanted to come out, but I dissuaded them. It was probably not the best idea, looking back. I would suggest definitely having the support of family around. Lesson positively learned! I felt at the time that my new L.A. friends were my family, and they did an incredible job of taking care of me.

The day of the surgery came. I was a champ. That lymph-node biopsy thing hurt like hell, but the surgery that followed was a breeze. Afterward, the physician told me that they had only removed four lymph nodes, and he was extremely confident that they had dissected all of the cancer from my body. I was in the recovery room for about forty-five minutes… and I was ready to get out of there, and put this behind me. Even the recovery room nurse was amazed at how quickly I came back to life, started chewing ice, and requested to leave. A very dear friend took me in the morning and then took care of me all day long, calling my sister and my parents with the latest news while I was in surgery. She was an angel to me… and still is.

The next two weeks, until my next appointment with the oncologist, when we would affirm radiation or chemo, seemed to coast by with the nights turning into days, turning into nights again. I had never watched so much TV and/or movies in my life. It was humbling for the first few days, as my roommate and his bf had to shower me for the first few days because I could not lift my arms due to the fact that the actual lymph nodes removed were taken from underneath my armpits. For this reason, I could barely take a shower, but I definitely could not dry myself off…yes, it was embarrassing, but they remain my close friends to this very day. I was home from work for one whole week. Almost everyone in my office came to visit me at home that week… the amount of support I received from friends and family was touching.

I ate lots of junk food, lots of pizza, lots of take-out, etc. I was on heavy amounts of Vicodin, so I really couldn't focus too much on the internet. I must say, people have unique reactions to learning a friend has cancer. Some of my friends disappeared upon hearing the news, while others became closer. I learned to have no judgments toward them… I just distanced myself a bit. I was still relatively okay with everything that was going on. At least, it felt that on some level, I had accepted what was going on. I was just in a pleasant state of denial. You gotta love the denied acceptance of it all!

It seemed at first as if everyone around me was having a much tougher time than I was with the bad news. In fact, so much so, that I, on several occasions, had to comfort other people through *their* healing process. In speaking with other cancer survivors, I have learned that this phenomenon is quite normal and happens much more frequently than you could imagine.

When I met with my oncologist two weeks after my surgery, his words moved me from **Mock-cceptance** into next stage of **Overwhelmdom**.

To Be Continued…

I Thought We Were Monogamous!

Just to refresh your memory, I had just arrived at the airport at midnight to my Paolo, his bff, and the long car ride home. It was dead silent. I mean, what was there to say, really? In those moments, it was more about just *being there* for him. There was nothing I could say or do to make him feel better, really… so I did all I could; I made small talk.

I was utterly exhausted from having done everything in my power to return home that night. Between my petrified state of worry that I would not make it home and the gynormous slew of emotions that had overcome me in those ten preceding hours, I had clearly overspent all my energy with an overwhelming concern for him. It was lovely to just be in a car with them. I could tell Paolo had been crying all day long. I had never seen him so distraught. I mean, if the test was decidedly not fallible, then, wow, he really was HIV+. It was still not computing with me. His bff was beat too. He looked beyond emotionally exhausted and it was a very, *very* long day for all of us.

The bff reluctantly dropped us off at the house. We both encouraged him to go home, get some rest, and then come back tomorrow evening for a Jewish Friday night dinner.

When Paolo and I were all alone, we hugged. Looking back, it was probably the longest embrace of our relationship. There was hurt, sadness, disappointment, regret and fear all boiled into one five-minute-long hug. Sometimes words just cannot express emotion like good physical contact can. This hug was so important not only to him and to me, but also to our relationship, and to the new challenge that we faced. I reassured him that I was going absolutely nowhere, that I loved him, and that we would do everything possible to get through this and come out on the other side. Obviously, I had done some research and found out that people who contract HIV nowadays have a great chance of living thirty years plus. And, really, from the point of view of a gay man in his prime, who wants to be older than sixty or seventy anyway? (Just kidding!)

That night... we feel asleep on the couch, which was not uncommon. I would usually wake up at one or two in the morning, wake him up, and we would both barely make it to the bedroom and fall sleep in an instant. It was a very sweet ritual. This time, though, we stayed there the whole night. The night flew by in a jiff. Before I knew it, it was morning. Time to get up. Time to brush our teeth. Time to shower. Time to put clothes on. One step at a time. One hour at a time. One minute at a time. That's what it took for those next five days. (Pardon the fragmented sentences, but they are representative of how I could only handle one action at a time literally those first few days.)

At the physician's office, we were happy to discover that our medical clinic was actually the number one medical group for Poz patients in Los Angeles. Our doctor was incredible. We both took more tests. He stayed with us for as long as we needed to process. I wanted all the information in the world on the subject. I wanted to educate myself as fast as I could, so I could be helpful to Paolo in explaining exactly what we were dealing with or what we could expect. After listening intently to the next steps and the forthcoming tests that would be administered after this initial round of testing, we must have walked out like zombies. Oh, yeah, and we clearly weren't allowed to have ANY type of sex with one another or anyone else until otherwise instructed. We weren't allowed to share razors, toothbrushes, nose-hair clippers, tweezers, even soaps. "Zombie" is a great word to describe what we each felt like at that point.

We decided to tell no one until we knew if I was positive or negative. We would find out by Wednesday of the following week, so only five days. Five days never seemed so long! All of the feelings rushed back from my three-day wait for the gosh-darn results for the cancer tests. It was the same icky, non-focused feeling that would paralyze anyone under the same circumstances. Needless to say, we watched a ton of movies, a great deal of *Sex and The City* re-runs, because he was a complete fanatic, and we spent oodles of time with his bff and partner, who had come home on an "emergency" from his Vegas Cirque du Soleil production. I could not have made it through those first few days without them. Their support was integral to my courage, support, and love.

No matter what we did, no matter where we were, there was that feeling of doom in the air. We were coasting. More importantly, I was coasting through the motions and the actions and behaviors of every day life, just never getting very far. We barely left the house during those few days. Monday. Long. Tuesday. Longer. Wednesday... was the longest. I kept texting the doctor asking for my results. He kept saying any day now. On Wednesday, however, Paolo's second round of results had come back. The numbers were even higher than the original. This meant that he not only had contracted HIV, but that it was spreading like wildfire, and he needed to be placed on a meds regime quickly. At this point, I believe that we started to toy with the FACT that our lives had *already* changed completely, without any warning. We were soon about to learn just how much. And, I'm sure, from an outsider's view, we must have appeared like zombies, embedded in our process of accepted denial.

Wednesday came and went. Instead of focusing on my results, we dealt with my Paolo and his feelings. Thursday... still nothing. On Friday, I was starting to get angry. Finally, the doctor called me in the middle of a movie (when obviously I left the theater) and told me, "You are negative." I asked, "Are you sure? Should I come in and get tested again?" He said that yes, it was for sure and no, I did NOT need to come in again. "You are very lucky, Seth." I was like, no shit, Sherlock! I hung up the phone and bowed my head for approximately five minutes, thanking God. Then it hit me. Oh God! I have a lot to deal with now... and how did he contract it, if I didn't? Did he cheat on me? Was it that three-way? And if he has had it for over five weeks, how the hell *didn't I get it?* Let's face it, I thought we were in a committed relationship, so *we* weren't careful with regard to protection and we had actually had sex a few times in that five-week period. Wow! I was one lucky son of a you-know-what, wasn't I? That's why I always believe there's got to be a higher purpose for me. I mean, in my research, I discovered that the highest risk for passing on the virus is in the first few months when treatment has not yet been administered.

Let me explain. For those of you who don't know, once you contract HIV, your body immediately develops antibodies and deploys them throughout the body. They usually measure those antibodies per cubic milliliter of blood plasma. This measurement is usually referred to as the "viral load". When Paolo was first tested, his count was already at 2,000,000 antibodies per cubic milliliter of blood. The doctor indicated that according to the rates of growth of antibodies, Paolo was most likely exposed to the virus 3-4 weeks prior to the date of testing. Within one week, his viral load dramatically increased from 2,000,000 to 8,000,000. The higher the viral load, the more risk you are to pass on the HIV virus. If treatment is administered, these numbers reduce tremendously to the amount of eighty (80) antibodies per cubic milliliter of blood, which is now considered to be "undetectable." At that point, you pose very little risk in transferring the virus to someone else, but there still is potential risk. If treatment is not administered, these numbers continue to grow higher and higher and your body will get weaker and weaker.

It was not until I received the news that I was HIV negative that I actually began to accept what was going on… and that's when all of the emotions started…the intensity and **Overwhelmdom**. Once I picked up my head and returned to the movie, within an instant, all of the feelings that I had been suppressing or negating came to the surface… It was not pleasant at all. In fact, it truly sucked. I had been so deeply upset and literally depressed over those few days, that now I had to put those feelings in a safe place for a rainy day and concentrate on Paolo. Don't get me wrong, I was negative, which felt amazing and incredible. However, Paolo was still positive. We still had to continue with separate razors, toothbrushes, soaps, nose-hair clippers, etc.… Our lives would remain forever altered. No matter how much I supported him in his journey, it was still tough.

To Be Continued…

Un Secuestro en México – A Kidnapping in Mexico

Kissing the DFW airport ground is no small feat, let me tell you! To remind you, it was 24 hours after the near kidnapping, and I had just landed on American soil. After literally kissing the airport floor, I texted my parents and my sister, as I customarily did when I returned to US territory so they would know I made it. (I knew I would not tell them about the day of terror in Mexico for at least a few weeks, if not months.) I was beyond grateful to have first, landed in the airport, and second, to be alive. The **Shock** had subsided and I began to feel just how complex, absurd, and potentially dangerous yesterday had been. Instead of freaking out, I held tightly to the fact that I was alive. I have always **Embraced** one truth about that unique and scary event – that I survived to tell the whole world about it.

I have never until this moment ever considered any "What ifs"? I do NOT allow myself to think about the "What ifs" with regard to this situation, because frankly all other alternatives would have been horrendous and even more damaging and painful. I truly believe it would make the experience that much harder to surrender and accept. I knew from the very beginning it was best for my growth and inner-happiness to NOT question what happened, and BELIEVE that everything happens for a purpose. I was able to do so, until my Head of Security/good friend was kidnapped the following month by the Zetas. (I will expound upon that in the next chapter, **Overwhelmdom**).

As for what happened to me, I cannot tell you the purpose even to this day. Was it to help me identify with victims of kidnapping?

No, I think the purpose for me was to share my story, open me up a little more, and cause extraordinary growth in my human understanding. (Those forty-five minutes of cartel time was just as scary as when I was traveling through Colombia on a bus, and was pulled over by guerrillas at 1am, with a shotgun aimed right at my head. Another story for another time...)

Sometimes we do stupid things and sometimes those stupid things turn out well. In my example, a stupid (but serious) threat, somehow miraculously worked in my favor. Yet it could have easily and quickly turned the other way. I'm honestly surprised they didn't take the armored vehicle, or me.. I was a very lucky individual on that day. Most of these thoughts crossed my mind after I kissed the DFW airport floor. I can't even begin to tell you about all of the awkward looks I received filled with disgust and utter amazement, at the site of me kissing the floor, but I didn't care at all. If they had known what I had witnessed the day before, they would have understood!

At the end of every LAX – MEX – LAX trip, there was always one point where I knew I was safe and one moment when I knew I was 100% secure – stepping into my Lincoln Town car or Lincoln Navigator. Yuri, a fabulous Ukrainian man, owned "Meridian Limo" in West Hollywood. I became friendly with him over the two years of traveling back and forth. He would take me to the airport and bring me home from the airport. The moment that I literally collapsed in his luxurious vehicle, I took a giant breath and exhaled with a massive sigh of relief. Oddly enough, even when I think about that day of terror now, I take a big breath of relief. That particular day, August 12, I probably took one of the biggest breaths of my entire life (okay, a bit dramatic, but I happen to be serious!)... big inhale and big exhale. Wow!

Customarily there would be a bit of chitchat between Yuri and me, but that day I wanted to be silent. Yuri had this uncanny ability to discern when I wanted to speak and when I wanted to remain silent. And so, that day, we rode the whole way in silence. He understood.

At this point, I was living by myself in West Hollywood. It was my favorite apartment to date, and when I stepped in the door, it was like never before. I'm telling you all of this because even though one can be in the stage of denied acceptance, I truly believe that the senses are heightened by about a hundred times. Everything seems sweeter, tastes better, looks more beautiful… perhaps it's because you are living so much so in the present that your perception of reality has heightened. To be honest, all I wanted was a hug from my new-ish boyfriend.

He probably arrived at my apartment about thirty minutes after me, and probably was a little scared himself. I gave him one of the longest hugs of our relationship definitely up to that point. I just wanted to feel safe. That evening, I was unusually quiet (for me) and he also became unusually quiet. He had no idea what to say to me. Can you blame him? Even though he had always made jokes about coming to find me if I were kidnapped, neither of us really thought something like this would ever happen.

For the next two weeks, unknowingly, I wasn't consumed by what had happened to me. I downplayed the event to my parents and sister only because prior to that point everyone kept encouraging me to quit that job ASAP and I still wasn't ready to quit an awesome executive position. For two weeks, I watched a TON of TV. I worked as little as possible, worked out as much as possible, ate regular and healthy meals, enjoyed going out, still enjoyed sex, and things were for the most part, back to normal. Thank you, **Mock-cceptance**.

At that point, I had no idea that once again, I was in **Mock-cceptance**. I actually proactively took advantage of this accepting time to work on this book like a crazy person. Consumed by the idea that I was close to the end, I ferociously made some great strides and headway. Although I wasn't quite ready to write about what had just happened to me, I could write about everything else that had happened in or having to do with Mexico. I was extremely productive during those two weeks.

Granted, everyone has his or her own journey and everyone's journey will be slightly different. However, everyone will go through this phase where everything seems like usual. In reality, it is just the body or mind's way of letting the news sink in slowly and for certain, letting the mind adjust itself to the recent event. Then, the reality hits you suddenly and brutally.

To Be Continued…

The Day Manhattan Stood Still

I was in mourning. My friends were in mourning. Hell, the whole wide world was in mourning. The first three days after 9/11 were indescribably trying. I felt a little numb. I felt very sad. I really couldn't talk to anyone or go anywhere. All New Yorkers were still in **Shock** and on Thursday of that week, I returned to work. After watching CNN for 72 hours straight, and sleeping very little, I was done seeing the collapsing, listening to the commentators, hearing the heroic stories and counting the missing people. I had had enough. As someone who sometimes feels every story, every obstacle, and every feeling for those sharing their tales, I was feeling their sadness, hurt, and **Shock** over and over again… and I just needed a break.

If you remember, we still had to get that shipment out. I remember that all of the Southbound Manhattan trains were stopping at Canal Street, so from that point South, one had to walk. There was the first line of demarcation at Canal Street. There was a second one, which stopped all traffic except for those that lived there, which was closer to the W.T.C. itself.

Curious beyond belief, there was smoke still rising from the W.T.C. area. I was taking a short pit- stop on the way to the "sweatshop" when I ran into my friend, Danny, from high school. I knew that he was living in N.Y.C. and we had tried to get together a couple of times, although unsuccessfully. His face perfectly expressed what I was feeling, utter numbness and **Shock**. We spoke for a couple of minutes before he told me that he had been working in one of the towers and shared his chilling story with me. My story wasn't nearly as exciting or as traumatic as his. Since we both grew up in the same small town in New Hampshire, he advised me that he was going back to Moultonborough for a few months to regroup. At that point, I wouldn't have minded going home for some much needed r&r, myself. He definitely had the right idea. I'm sure he might not remember that chance encounter, but I do, like it was yesterday. Again, heightened senses.

As we went our separate ways, I looked around me – the landscape was bare. There were hardly any people out walking. Usually at this time in the morning, there would be hundreds upon hundreds of people out on Canal Street… but it was a ghost town. It was terrifying to me. I had a job to do, though, and, by golly, we were going to get those boxes out!

Entwined over these first few days after the attack, I was fascinated and captivated by all the news coverage. As easy as it was to believe that the Twin Towers collapse was just another movie on tv, something inside me told me it wasn't happening to me, but to someone else. I felt estranged from the events and distanced from my norm. Yet, I wasn't sad. Everything felt copasetic and okay. Thus, the reason I was even able to return to work. That, and I knew people were counting on me.

Everyone in the sweatshop including myself worked harder than ever to complete that assignment. I imagine it was because we were so devastated that we needed something to do, so as to focus all of that strange energy that kept filling up our minds.

It was about three to four days after the collapsing of the Twin Towers that my **Mock-cceptance** ended. Most of you are not going to like this...but my **Mock-cceptance** ended when the stench of evaporated and burnt human waste hit our street, 54th Street. That is when, the intensity and **Overwhelmdom** hit me, and the rest of New York.

To Be Continued...

A Friend Taken Too Young

A stellar example of **Mock-cceptance** is how I felt when one of my closest friends in the world passed away in March of 2003. My friend Luli was one of the greatest people I knew. Sure, she made mistakes and dated some losers, but who hasn't, right? I should start at the beginning, so that you can fully understand how traumatic her loss was for me.

Luli and I first met on a dark and stormy day, in dance class. Seriously, it was dark and stormy. By the way, did I mention that we were in Quito, Ecuador? Technically, we met at the Universidad de San Francisco, in Cumbaya, Ecuador, just outside the capital city of Quito in August of 1997 and there were always thunderstorms rumbling through that area. Yes, in college, I was a great dancer and choreographer. Would you doubt me for a second? We met on my very second day of school there. I had studied French since junior high school, and had only taken one year of Spanish, but my Spanish was solid. Luli, short for Maria de Lourdes, had studied in the United States for a year in high school, and her English was amazing. We hit it off immediately.

She and her adorable sister, Majo, short for Maria Jose, lived about five blocks away from me in the neighboring metropolis of Quito. I would usually ride the city bus in the morning, to ensure I was there on time… which was always an interesting experience, especially considering I came home infected with fleas three times from the stupid chickens that people carried on the bus with them. (Never did I imagine fifteen years later would I ever be the proud papa to four hens.) Anyway, every Tuesday and Thursday, after dance class, Majo, Luli, and I would carpool home together and, from there, our relationship flourished.

Majo had also studied for a year in the United States somewhere, and her English was also excellent. Early on, I informed them that I only wanted them to speak to me in Spanish until after the first month or so. And, boy, did they keep to that promise! I have to admit these wonderful sisters definitely taught me everything I know about Castellano (that is, a derivative of the Spanish from Spain) and then some. They would constantly correct me, tell me jokes, and play silly little word games and verbal riddles, but they never *ever* gave up on me. Thanks to them and my loving Escobar-Peñaherrera host family, with whom I lived for nine months, my Spanish became awesome.

During my time in Ecuador, I hung out mostly with "the sisters" and my Ecuadorean host family. I still remain in contact with this unbelievably warm, sincere, and beyond generous family. I thought that *my* family was close, but my Ecuadorean family was the closest family I had ever experienced. They pretty much spent every day with one another as well as the entire weekends together. My host mom and dad had grandchildren my age, and I called them what the grandkids called them, Mamá Pepita and Papá Lucho. The grandkids were there, joining us for lunch and dinner, almost every day. We all laughed together, cried together, and drank way too much together. It was a super tight-knit family, in which it was extremely easy to assimilate myself fully. They all welcomed me like a family member, and vice versa. They have often told me out of all of their exchange students, I was the family's absolute favorite and the most loved.

Majo and Luli were my confidants and best friends. They could tell I was gay from the very first moment, and it was as if they accepted me even more than if I were a straight guy. I obviously could tell no one in Ecuador that I was gay, so to be 100% myself in front of them was an incredible safety. Finita and Petico (their parents) were also incredible individuals and embraced me as their son from the very first moment I arrived on the scene.

The friendship blossomed. We were inseparable... except when Luli would see her loser of an American boyfriend... but that just gave Majo and I time to talk, share, see movies, etc. See, I was rich in Ecuador, in 1997 - 1998. Two hundred dollars per month allowed all of us to do a great many things, anytime we wanted.

They confided in me about tons of things as did in them. They allowed me to experience firsthand what true friendship meant and 100% unconditional love between friends. They were truly incredible. As the months progressed, our relationships became more like brothers and sisters than friends. I even slept over at their house, many a late night, always falling asleep in their beds, and then Petico would always come in and offer me the guest bedroom. It was hilarious. He had no idea at that point! Ah, fond memories!

At the university, second semester, we all took a course entitled "Sexuality & Attraction", the discussions of which I was the only American with good enough Spanish to participate and so, naturally, I became the American spokesperson for the class. The teacher, a Canadian-born therapist was intrigued by my gayness and we started having sessions wherein she tried to "discover" the reason that I was gay. She was apparently trying to "cure" me. Indeed, I found it rather amusing, so I politely went with it.

When we came upon the lesbian and gay chapters in the textbook (in late April), it was time for me to "come out" and become the gay expert for the class as well. Majo and Luli stood behind me the entire time. They would help within the class; if I were stammering or if I were embarrassed, they would *always* be there for me. Coming out in Ecuador is not an easy task. At that point, it was still very dangerous for anyone to come out of the closet. I knew that within a few days, the entire school would know and therefore my life could possibly be in danger. Majo and Luli never waned in their support of me. So much so, in fact, that they told some of their huskier and more popular guy friends to definitely keep an eye on me and protect me, if anything should happen. And, amazingly enough, because they really respected me, those big and burly men did kept their promise to the girls.

For our end-of-the-year project in that class, we three worked together to discovery the levels of truth, honesty, and public opinion about gayness in the three major colleges/universities in Quito. We polled individuals, for which we'd get slack at times, but "my gals" would always defend me and the gayness until the bitter end. I remember one time when we were handing out questionnaires at a local college, a group of three guys snatched the surveys from me, tore them to shreds, and started calling me "maricón" (faggot in Spanish). Luli immediately ran up to them saying, "How do we know you are not gay? Are you scared to come out to your friends? Are you gay?" They proceeded to run away from us, literally terrified of Luli. "Oooooh, look who's scared now! Maricones!!!" It was absolutely hilarious, especially as they ran off with their tails between their legs. That was my Luli!

Majo and Luli helped me survive one of the most harrowing times in my life when I actually feared for my physical wellbeing. They were always proud and honored to be my ñañas. "Ñañas" is the traditional Quechuan (native Latin American) word for "sisters"… and that they definitely were. I can't express to you how much their friendship and support meant to me throughout those last couple weeks when word finally broke out in the university that I was gay.

Our investigation into the constitutional laws surrounding sexual orientation for our homosexuality project was so in-depth that we met the head of the Lesbian, Gay, Bisexual and Transgender Union (would be equivalent to the head of the Human Rights Campaign), who, of course, had a crush on me. I'm not gonna lie. He was very cute! We learned that Ecuador was, in fact, the second country in the world to include sexual orientation in their constitution, to protect the rights of gays in 1998. Meeting the Head of the Union was a big day for us all. In fact, after we finished the project, Luli and Majo were proud to have taken part in the start of the gay rights movement not just in the university but also in the country of Ecuador. They had never been a part of anything remotely like that.

As I mentioned, I was the first out gay person in our university, then another followed, then another. It continued to inspire more gays to come out in the years following as well. It was Ecuador, people, in 1998! Even though sexual orientation was a group protected by their constitution, we were still at risk for being physically hurt. Religious views take many, many years to change. Apparently, a lot has changed since, but let me tell you, when I was there, the gay bars were underground and you needed secret codes to get in. It was a scary time for me. I had never, nor have I ever, been as scared of being beaten up or killed for my gayness. Thank God for those girls!

As my friendship with Luli was blossoming, when I would see her from across the campus, I would yell at the top of my lungs: Maria de Lourdes!!! But I mean at the top of my lungs… and she would yell Seth Santoro at the top of her lungs. It was our special greeting… we were crazy and twenty years old. It was fun…

and I miss her. I had no idea that as much as I needed them in my life, they also needed me in theirs. I'll explain that part in the chapters to come.

Back to the night I found out she passed away. The night I found out that she had passed away, as I said previously, I tried everything I could to find a flight to get me there in time for the funeral at 10:30 the next morning, but I just couldn't arrive before 12pm. And that was on an international air-cargo flight. It was horrible. It was just horrible. I figured since I couldn't make the funeral, I would plan to go down 3-4 weeks later, when all the dust had settled and when they would need some fun and relaxing Seth time.

When I telephoned Majo later at home to tell her my plan, she was out. As I was leaving a message, Mamá Finita picked up the phone. Oh, God. I was not prepared at all for that. I had NO idea what to say in English, let alone in Spanish. This poor woman, who had had a pretty rocky relationship over the years with Luli, had now lost her eldest daughter forever. I told her about the fact that I wanted so badly to be there, but I just couldn't make the funeral. She completely understood. She held it together on the phone until I told her I would be down to see her within the next month. She gasped for air... and said (in Spanish, of course), "My little Luli has died, Seth, what am I going to do? My little Luli has died." Ahem...what do you say to that? Granted, I had kept up with my Spanish, but what I said wasn't nearly as perfect as what I would have said in English. I said something to the effect of, "I know, I know. God must have better plans for her... maybe as our angel."

You need to know something else; Mamá Finita was deeply religious and spiritual and I knew I would have to say something big, poignant, and fast because this woman loved me as a son and I was one of her daughter's best friends. It was a lot of pressure to put on me, but I bounced back with resolve and poise. She responded amazingly well to my words. She confirmed with me that I would for sure be coming down to see her soon, to which I responded of course... and I said, my thoughts, love, and prayers are with you... they will be with you tomorrow and with you always. I will see you soon.

When I hung up the phone, I nearly collapsed. It was one of the most challenging and emotionally-charged conversations I had ever had. I honestly cannot imagine losing a child. To be honest, it is my biggest fear in this world. Majo contacted me not too long after that, with sadness and a heavy heart... she also understood that it was probably better for me to go down to Ecuador in a couple of weeks, when they could focus on me and we could focus on family. I ended up spending the weekend with my grandparents... and although I was terribly sad, I didn't cry. They were very understanding and sometimes we just sat in silence, which was okay too.

No one could figure out why I hadn't broken down yet. To be honest, at the time, I felt amazingly resolved with her passing. Of course, that wasn't the case, but it was this **Mock-cceptance** phase that totally overran my life for two weeks. Yup, it took me two weeks before my mind, body, and soul were ready to deal with her death. Wait until you hear what happened... it was like a scene out of a movie...

To Be Continued...

5 THINGS TO REMEMBER WHEN IN MOCK-CCEPTANCE

1. Ask for Support from Those Around You.

If this has anything to do with your health, ALWAYS take someone else along to listen to what the doctor is saying. You will listen and hear all of the words, but after the word "cancer" or "HIV," you (or the patient) won't hear much else. Your mind will draw a blank and you won't be able to recall anything. Do yourself a favor, and just take someone else with you!

2. Pick a Project. Complete a Task. Or Create Something.

Make a list of all the projects / tasks you have been procrastinating doing in your apartment, house, or bedroom and then perhaps do one or two of them. Take advantage of the perfect time to start the task or even finish a task that's been waiting for you. You might actually feel productive. We like productive!

3. No Major Decisions.

Now is probably not the best time to make a tough decision. Whether it is about work, love, friends, or family, it's not a good time. Even though you may feel great, it is an illusion of the mind. Take that time and instead focus on you and what you need.

4. Speak Your Mind.

Be authentic and tell people what you need. People really do not know what you are thinking or feeling. Be honest and tell them the truth. If you need someone to just sit with you in silence, tell them. If you need someone to come over and cook dinner for you, ask them. If you tell them what you need, people have a better idea of how to help.

5.   Find Gifts from the Universe.

Seek hints or gifts from the universe that you are in the right place at the right time. In other words, that you are supposed to be exactly where you are. As I was running for that second plane in Mexico, and desperately worried about making my connection flight, for the first time ever they handed me a little boarding pass with a number on it. The number was my absolute favorite number, 24. I knew then that no matter how much pain or challenging hours were about to come, I was in the right place at the right time. Signs are all around us at all times. The fun is in finding them.

MOCK-CCEPTANCE - In Conclusion:

"I'm Fine!" - **Mock-cceptance**, the second important step in the Smile From The Inside S.M.I.L.E. model, is part-denial and part-acceptance. Hence the name, **Mock-cceptance**. It really does feel like you may be on top of the world. It gives you the false sense of security that everything is A-okay, even though everything is heightened around you. You remarkably feel that everything is going to be all right... and perhaps you don't even need to be sad or grieve or feel angry or any emotion, for that matter. As I have explained, it is the mind-body connection allowing the terrible information time to adjust or to trickle into your system. Once the trickling has completed, it usually takes a trigger moment or a trigger event for you to actually move into the next phase: **In Overwhelmdom**, where anything can happen... and every possible feeling will and does come up.

Remember, don't beat yourself up for not having more emotions or feeling like you are not dealing with what's going on. Enjoy the **Mock-cceptance**. It will get challenging pretty quickly and it will get tough. Give yourself the time your mind and body need to adjust and make the necessary arrangements for the next step to occur all on its own. Everything will happen in due course. Don't go forcin' nothin'... because that won't get you anywhere. Just be with your feelings or lack thereof and just be lazy in your denial.

Trust me. **Mock-cceptance** is a very unique time in the S.M.I.L.E. Method of healing. No matter if everything is heightened, your mind and body are going through something mighty big. They are dealing with it the only way they know how. Trust that your mind, body, and soul know what they are doing. After all, they have thousands of years of evolution behind them. This stuff is not easy. There are so many layers and colors. It rarely gets any easier, either. Life has already changed. Life has already moved forward with or without your approval.

Mock-cceptance is similar to the Sun Salutations in yoga or the first two hundred repetitive crunches in an abs class. Even though you have done these exercises a million times (and may be on autopilot, as suggested earlier), it is conditioning your body from the inside. This is where the juices start flowing in the class and, similarly, in the Smile From The Inside process. This is where it starts getting good and the hard work lies just ahead. As you begin to overcome the denial phase (**Mock-cceptance**), your mind and body start literally acknowledging the emotional and physical reaction to the event(s), thus leading to the next phase of **In Overwhelmdom,** wherein your emotions go everywhere. **Mock-cceptance** is the second necessary step we all must journey through to live an easier Smile From The Inside way of life.

IN OVERWHELMDOM

STAGE THREE: IN OVERWHELMDOM.
Emotions

noun

1. Emotions are a reaction, both psychological and physical, subjectively experienced as strong feelings, many of which prepare the body for immediate action.

2. Emotions are transitory, with relatively well-defined beginnings and endings.

3. Certain emotions themselves, considered to be primary emotions – joy, anger, sadness, fear, and love – are thought to be innate, while complex emotions – such as altruism, shame, guilt, and envy – seem to arise from social learning.

4. In daily life, emotional arousal may have beneficial or disruptive effects, depending on the situation and the intensity of the emotion. Moderate levels of arousal increase efficiency levels by making people more alert. However, intense emotions – either positive or negative – interfere with performance because central nervous system responses are channeled in too many directions at once. The effects of arousal on performance depend on the difficulty of the task at hand; emotions interfere less with simple tasks than with more complicated ones[9].

Expressed Feeling = "Ugh!"

Yes, I invented the word, **Overwhelmdom**. I think it's the perfect word. It is the place (hence "dom") where overwhelming emotions take over. See above for what the experts say about emotions and overwhelming emotions. Great. That's exactly it. Those intense and poignant emotions are exactly what I am referring to **In Overwhelmdom**. And here is where the real work begins.

In this stage of Smile From The Inside, you have begun the gynormous task of dealing with the newly received information. **Ugh** is the best way to describe it. You have no patience for B.S. This is when you start to see things perhaps in black and white. This part is uncomfortable... to the max! This is where the emotions start to roar inside. Anger. Hurt. Depression. Doubt. Worry. The self (a.k.a. the ego) has been wounded and the repercussions are intense. Both anger and depression come from a feeling of

---

9   "Emotions" Beins, Bernard, Feldman, Alan J., and Gall, Susan, *The Gale Encyclopedia of Psychology*, Gale, 1996.

being hurt or betrayed. All of these emotions are valid, normal, and affecting.

There are two choices here **In Overwhelmdom**: the first is to go deep into the anger and depression and stay there for a while, or the second is to acknowledge your irritation and sadness, and ride the wave of poignant emotions like a champ. The choice is yours. Either way, you will experience the emotions of anger, hurt, and depression, the so-called primary emotions. It just depends on how much you let them affect you. Sometimes this choice will feel involuntary, sometimes deliberate. There are some individuals among us who can actually choose their emotions (I wish I were better at this phenomenon). From a spiritual perspective, this is completely possible for everyone. From a more pragmatic standpoint, good luck to the rest of us!

The ability to choose your emotions is based on years of conditioning, from birth until the present, the circumstances you have been dealt, and the stability or instability of your childhood experience. Ask yourself how adaptive and acceptive (isn't that a nice word?) you have become to the realities that surround you and have occurred to you lately. How well you deal with these situations will determine whether you control your emotions or you let your emotions control you. Remember, there's nothing negative about being sad, angry, or depressed. Think about that for a second. All of these emotions are helpful in understanding just where you are at any minute, like a built-in barometer. This intense and captivating bout of emotions is when you are **In Overwhelmdom**.

Hold on to your seats, folks, 'cause it's gonna get bumpy! The overwhelming emotions are out of this world! It is not pretty. It is not a hallmark card, nor a sunny day. In fact, it seems like the weight of the world is all around you. This is tough. This is uncomfortable. This is not usually a good time. If you can create the space you need to just "be" for a while, take the opportunity to do so.

If you are the type of person that needs to "get it out" or "let it out" - by all means, do so… ideally, with someone else. Just make sure it's not with the person with which you have the drama. Ideally, choose someone who loves you unconditionally and offers no judgment. Once again, this stage shall pass. I promise you will get over this. Sometimes (as in the case of myself), you don't even know when you begin to land **In Overwhelmdom**.

You will soon begin to recognize this stage from the outside-in and better understand how to help support yourself and your journey toward Smile From The Inside living. If **Shock** starts the warm-up and movement by the mind and body, and **Mock-cceptance** is the mental and physical conditioning and practice that get your juices flowing, then **In Overwhelmdom** ignites the emotional superhighway where you and your emotions get pushed to the absolute limits. Through the furtherance of my intimate stories in this chapter, you will see how **In Overwhelmdom** sits at center stage in the S.M.I.L.E. Method for healing. Without this overwhelming charge of emotions, you cannot proceed to the last two stages.

Um… You Lost Me At Cancer

When I left off last, my oncologist was happy with the surgery and thought it was a complete success. Since he was so optimistic about the whole thing, I decided to take his word for it. It was not until two weeks later, when I met with the doctor to review the physical healing and the results of the additional tests from the day of the surgery, that I discovered I had been in the **Mock-cceptance** phase. When thoughts of doubt would creep in, I would quickly reassure myself not to worry until there was something to worry about. Or, I would think about my last conversation with the oncologist and how confident he was to have removed all of the cancer and that it hadn't spread to other areas. Okay. I won't worry now.

Just the word *chemo* scares me. I've seen it first hand. I've seen what it can do. It is no joke. The word, *radiation*, doesn't sound much better, but it's easier to tolerate. Either way, it would be challenging, but I would get through it. I figured since it was Stage I cancer (that's what I was told), the chances of having radiation or chemo were small. Nonetheless, when we returned to the John Wayne Cancer Institute two weeks later, I was sweating profusely, nauseated, and had quite the army of nerves flowing through my entire body.

I have always felt a great deal of sadness in hospitals. It's not that I'm scared of them at all, but it's very heavy energy for me. Since the John Wayne Cancer Institute is actually within St. John's Hospital in Santa Monica, California, we always passed by the hospital lobby. On that particular date, as we signed in, I noticed this poor woman who seemed very sick and nearing the end of her life, at first glance. It appeared that she was with her husband and two kids, who were playing in the kids' section of the waiting room. Our eyes met with a gentle acknowledgement and she immediately asked what type of cancer I had. I responded that I had an aggressive form of skin cancer, however, they were pretty certain they had removed it all two weeks ago, including a few lymph nodes.

Since she had asked me the question, I thought it was only fair and appropriate that I return the courtesy, if you will. She told me that her cancer was extremely rare, and that it was eating away at her from the inside out. I was mortified. The husband looked so depressed. Of course, I said to myself, Wow! Comparatively speaking, I should be on top of the world, right? She was very quick to respond, however, that everyone has his or her own cancer and that we never can be certain of how severe vs. non-severe a cancer can be. She immediately wanted me to know that my "suffering" was just as valid as hers. I still disagree. I'm pretty sure she is no longer alive now, and I managed to heal, continue in remission for *six* years now (knock on wood), and have a great story of myself and my cancer. Wow! Everyone has his or her story.

After more blood tests, weight tests, etc., they placed me in the "holding" room where I was told my oncologist would be in a few minutes. Those ten minutes felt like *ten* lifetimes for me. Even though I was sitting with my bff, there was no comfort for me, no hiding, no evading the truth of this matter. I tried to find magazines, make small talk, do whatever I could to focus on anything other than myself. Nothing would work.

When my oncologist entered the room, I had to hold the tears back. He was just as awesome as always - even-tempered, casual, and sympathetic. After making small talk and reviewing my scars, he said... you look good. I'll see you in three months, okay? I was like, "Um... excuse me... what about the cancer? Has it spread? Do I need radiation? Or chemo?" He looked at me and said, "Oh, we would have called you had anything been wrong with any of your tests results... didn't anyone tell you that?" No, they most certainly had not called me! My heart dropped to the floor. I gave him a huge hug, then I started to cry. It was time.

It was definitely time for me to cry. It was time for me to let go of everything that I was holding onto inside. I had needed to be strong for my friends and family up until that point - not anymore though. I needed to release. I needed to sit back, relax, and enjoy the show. There is a fabulous quote: "People cry, not because they are weak. It's because they've been strong for too long." – Sophie Giele. That was exactly my situation. It was rather a messy cry. It was one of those ugly cries. It was so filled with emotion that I couldn't even walk for a minute.

OMG... I had just averted chemo and radiation. I was going to live. For some reason, to me, cancer used to be a death sentence, and that's what secretly had been in the back of my mind the entirety of the three weeks prior. Those three weeks of anguish had led up to this moment. For all that time, there was a little part of me that had thought that I was going to die. It's normal. It happens to everyone. It makes complete sense. But that day, I learned that I wasn't going to die. In fact, I had about seventy more years to live.

I cannot quite express the release and the relief that I felt in those few moments. Up until that moment, it felt as if I was being squeezed by a rubber band... but then, all of a sudden, the tight rubber band was cut and the pressure was completely released! I felt like doing a jump for joy! At the same time, I simply could not catch my breath. Life, as I knew it, would never be the same. The sigh of relief had come over my mind, body, and soul. I was so tired of being strong and keeping myself together, that I unraveled right then and there. I was angry. I was sad. I was disappointed. I was ecstatic. I was elated. I was happy. I was going to live!

After taking a few minutes to compose myself, we left the hospital. Not only did I feel a huge release, but I also immediately felt an extreme range of other emotions. I was happy. I was angry. I was sad. I was upset. Of course, we had to stop off at Whole Foods to pick up my fave cookies... and there, from Whole Foods, I called my mom and dad, my sister, my aunt, and my ex... all within a ten-minute span! The chocolate chip cookies were delicious... as always! The rawness I felt was crazy. Compared to the three weeks prior, I was feeling everything now – and I mean EVERYTHING.

There was a lot of anger inside of me. All of my friends can attest to the fact that I am not an angry individual, so this feeling was pretty foreign to me. On the way home, I began to understand why people have road rage. (I, myself, had never had road rage, but over the next couple of days, I would begin to understand those types of thoughts.) I was angry with God. I was angry at the universe. I was angry with my parents for letting me in the sun all those hours when I was a child playing by our lake. I was angry with myself. Needless to say, anything and everything angered me.

As the anger subsided, a few days later, the overwhelming feelings of sadness and depression arrived quickly and swiftly. It was *not* pretty. It was actually very disturbing to me. I was so sad. Nothing or no one could pull me out of it. Everything bothered me. Thus, the term **Overwhelmdom**. I had no patience at work. Simple things that would normally just slide by became events of enormity and drama. Little things that would happen at work would overwhelmingly annoy me. When asked what was going on with me, I would tell people that

I was having a delayed reaction of overwhelming feelings about my recent cancer. I was abrasive, emotional, and kinda crazy.

Some days I didn't know if I was sad, angry, green, red, blue, or black. Anyone who knows me knows that I like to wear bright colors, especially orange, which symbolizes spirituality and confidence. Truly beyond myself, it took me about three to four weeks to calm down, gain some type of equilibrium, and start wearing orange again. For those few weeks, though, I just went with it. I allowed the feelings to come and go. I did everything I could to minimize my outbursts of unmitigated hatred or sadness toward everything or everyone else. I watched a great deal of TV. I kept myself really busy… but I have learned that it is best to acknowledge what's going on and then just ride the ride… eat more junk food, work out, take drugs (kidding). When I was prescribed Vicodin for my under-shoulder pain, I will admit that I used some of the Vicodin, even when the pain wasn't so bad!

Overwhelmdom is the place where the mind, body, and soul finally agree you are ready to start dealing with whatever event has occurred. Be okay with ups and downs. Be okay with feeling every emotion possible. Be okay with allowing the process to continue. You deserve some time to yourself. This would also be a good time to take a few days off, which is exactly what my friends and I did. We went to The Bacara Resort in Santa Barbara, California for a spa-pampered weekend and some much needed r&r. It was incredible… and *very* much needed. In fact, we *all* needed it. It had been quite the month for all of us.

To Be Continued…

I Thought We Were Monogamous!

So, I was saying that my doctor had just told me that I was HIV negative. Ugh. I felt like my knees were going to give out. I just couldn't believe it. I mean, I really couldn't believe it. I questioned him several times if there could be any way that I could be positive by now. He maintained that as of such and such date, I did NOT show any signs of the HIV antibodies; there was no sign that I had been exposed to the virus. I still didn't believe him. I mean, Paolo and I had been physically intimate prior to his initial tests on multiple occasions, and, in my mind, there was a great chance that I could have contracted the virus. Wow! By some miracle of God, it must have been, I did not receive it. I might even admit that because of Paolo's intimacy issues and our decreased sexual interactions, my life may have been saved.

Remember, we were in the middle of a movie when the doctor called and told me the amazing news. I had left my phone on during the movie because I knew he could call or text at any minute. He texted, "Got your Results! Call me!" That was exactly what he texted me. And so I ran outside the movie theater and returned the call right away. The ten to fifteen seconds' lapse for the medical office to track him down felt like two eternities. The first thing he said was, "Seth? You're negative. All your tests came back negative!" I thought I was going to fall over. I couldn't breathe. I couldn't think. This was probably my train of thoughts at the time:

1) If I don't have it, then what the hell happened?

2) Could it be the third person involved in that three-way we had six weeks ago?

3) Oh My God… now I have to spend the rest of my life with him

4) As if our issues weren't bad enough, now we have to add on this

5) I could never leave him now; I won't desert him, I just won't

6) OMG, I don't have it. Then, what the hell happened?

7) He must have cheated on me

8) Wow… he's going to be so relieved that he didn't give it to me

9) Ugh… this is going to make it much worse for him

10) What? Am I immune? I must be immune?

(Now, there are actually people out there who are immune to certain strands of the HIV virus… I am convinced to this day that I am one of those people. I had to have been exposed to the virus.)

My thoughts and feelings were all over the place. He is going to be happy that he didn't give it to me. I am happy that he didn't give it to me. But, now what? Now, we have to live the rest of our lives with the HIV virus amongst us. I will always be negative and he will always be positive. At one moment, I would think that was special. The next moment, I would think that a preposterous thought. One thing in my mind was for sure: I would *not* leave him. It was never even a question in my mind until much later in time.

Then, the anger and sadness took over. Mind you, this was all in about thirty seconds. I was angry that he might have cheated on me. I was angry that he put my life in danger – even if he didn't know it. I was pissed that it would change the course of both of our lives, not just his. Now, we had to tell people. We had to tell my parents. We had to tell our friends... yuck! Yuck! Yuck! I didn't have the most pristine record of successful monogamy, but I had not cheated on Paolo. We were working so hard to be together and to share our lives together and now he goes and does this. That was probably about another thirty seconds. I'm sure I used much more inappropriate language in my mind. I was peeved.

I got it together, went back in the movie theater and gave a huge thumbs up to Paolo and his bffs that had spent pretty much the last ten days with us non-stop. They were and continue to be the best of friends with Paolo. Good people.

After sitting back down, I decided we would need to have a conversation about all of this later on. I still was in a complete state of **Shock** that I was negative. Sitting there, I couldn't really focus on the end of the movie. I don't even remember what movie it was. My mind and my heart were racing like nobody's business. I had basically averted an early death. The range of emotions was severe. I was elated, horrified, happy, sad, angry, relieved, etc.... I could not figure out which way was up... or down. It was truly beyond.

It was at that moment that I started to notice that there was a definite pattern for how I heal, and I came up with the word **Overwhelmdom**. Once again, I was in that place. That place where I had so many emotions, I couldn't keep track of them.

Oh yeah, and over the course of the next few days, I actually was having hot flashes and night sweats. We set up a makeshift bed in front of the TV in the living room. Our therapist later told us that this makeshift bed in the living room was a transitional place where we both felt safe. Sometimes, we would both have night sweats… him because of the new medicines and me because of the anxieties releasing from by body.

During this time when I was completely **In Overwhelmdom**, I was also taking care of Paolo as if he were my child. It was a terrible, terrible time. In contrast to the previous months, we had probably never felt as close as we did for those first few weeks. We were both extreme wrecks, but didn't fight at all. We were incredible to one another. There was definitely a lot of love and a lot of fear in both of our hearts. The crazy part is despite all of those emotions, for those few weeks, I was oddly able to keep my composure at all times. I suppose this time I was way more aware of my own healing process, and could therefore rein all of my emotions in when necessary. I suppose in some way, I was already practicing the awareness of my smiling from the inside.

As for those first few weeks, we did not leave the house much. We felt no need or impulse to be around other people. We did not want to "act" as if everything was okay. That's exhausting work too. We watched the "Sex and The City" complete series… two times in a row. We rented a bunch of movies, including "The Lord of The Rings" trilogy, and I think I may have forced him to watch all of the "Harry Potter" films.

What about work, you may ask? I did the absolute least I could for work, over those two weeks. At first, I could not focus very well on my responsibilities as Director, which were many. As time passed, work became a welcome distraction. Anything that distracted me from the intense **Overwhelmdom** was appreciated. It allowed me to take some much-needed breaths. Even as my emotions came and went, it was nice to get away from the reality of how HIV would forever be a part of our life.

Despite all of my emotions, I was in this with him for the long haul. I decidedly would never abandon him. I was there every day for him. I, as his boyfriend and domestic partner, made a commitment to take care of him through sickness and health, for better or worse. Some would say I am noble. Some would say I was stupid. I just didn't see any other options.

As you can probably guess, it was I who was doing all of the research and it was I separating his daily regimen of new anti-retroviral meds. I would tell him bits and pieces of what I had discovered and offered a few websites for him to check out, which, to me, seemed apropos for where he was in his evolution. Paolo never fact-checked any of the data. On occasion, he would rattle off to friends and family members the information that I had previously relayed to him. I let him have that... because, let's be honest, I really cannot imagine his process and his evolution of emotions. All I knew was that my emotions were all over the place, and it made sense to help him with the research.

As I was a bit more aware than Paolo of my own phases and process, while he may have remained in the dark, it became clear to me what I had to do in order to keep my sanity, keep from crying in public, and keep from lashing out at stupid people. In my experience, when you are **In Overwhelmdom**, it seems like people around you become more selfish and even stupid. Obviously, your threshold for physical pain, your patience, and just about anything decreases dramatically. The more you can recognize that you are in this stage, the more "control" you can have over the emotions. Remember, emotions are like farts, they just happen all the time!!! As I explained earlier, in this stage of emotional volatility, we do have a small choice whether to **Embrace** and celebrate the emotions or fight them all… each one. I say trust the process. Trusting the process means being present to what's going on inside while decidedly embracing your present and ultimately going with the flow. Trust that your mind and body know what they are doing. Celebrate that this too shall pass. If you choose to fight all of your emotions, you lose the awareness and can easily lose control of your feelings. You don't want to be a hot mess. You want to consciously choose when you want to be a hot mess! That is empowerment!

About two weeks after discovering that I was safe from HIV, we began to make lists of people to tell. People that must know and people that should know. Oh, no, I thought, my parents! Yikes! And that was how I started **Learning** to surrender to the idea that my partner in life was going to forever have HIV, and that's just the way it was going to be.

To Be Continued…

Un Secuestro en México – A Kidnapping in Mexico

That ONE day confirmed the fact that I would NEVER step foot inside Mexico again. Filled with assassinations, deaths, and kidnappings, Mexico was just too much for me to handle. The second half of the month of August was crazy busy. I was working virtually, more or less, and traveling for personal reasons. Around the first of September, my boss and I discussed whether or not returning to Mexico was too much to ask. He made it clear to me that my job required me to return to Mexico. I finally conceded that it was too much to handle and that if I could not perform that role from the California office, perhaps we should start talking about my transition plan out of that role. I did not want to quit at all, but I felt strongly that I would not return to Mexico. My job was in Mexico, and it just was not a good business practice to supervise a team of fifty people from two thousand miles away. It had proved hard enough traveling back and forth to Mexico for seven to ten days per month. There were a lot of questions from my team about when I was going to return to Mexico. I left their questions unanswered.

The truth was that there was *no way* that I was going to *ever* step foot in Mexico again. Two years later, it's still pretty hard for me to say that I would ever *choose* to return to Mexico. Ever.

After those initial conversations, the emotions started flying around again. I was definitely in a state of hypersensitive awareness. In fact, I was pretty jumpy for a few months. I started to have mood swings, which is very unusual for me. The range of intense emotions was severe. That is how I knew I was **In Overwhelmdom** and a little traumatized by the events in Mexico.

My new boyfriend at the time thought it would be best to get a dog. So, Maggie, the French bulldog, became my "emotional support" animal... and, boy, did she ever do a great job! She is still one of the most amazing creatures ever to have entered my life to this day.

A few weeks later, in early September, my nephew was born on a Friday night, on the East Coast, and I flew out that following Tuesday to meet the new addition to our family. My nephew was - and still is - the cutest thing ever. Unfortunately, on Wednesday morning at about 10am, I received a phone call from my boss saying that my Head of Security and good friend, Silvestre, had been taken. I'm sorry. What? Yes, he had been kidnapped. He was already in touch with the proper authorities and our security agency in Mexico was on red alert. There was nothing we could do but wait!

After a short and very succinct conversation, we hung up the phone, and everything finally hit me. I crazily ran to the bathroom and threw up. Really…I could not believe this was happening. I cannot believe this was my life. I cannot believe that I had almost been kidnapped and now poor Silvestre actually was. Oh God, I hope they don't kill him. I hope they don't murder him. I couldn't fathom what he must be going through right now.

Words could not describe how I felt on the inside. I was sick to my stomach. I was disgusted by my job, my life, Mexico, the Zetas, everyone. Honestly, I felt awful and that it was somehow my fault. The night prior, I had told Silvestre which vehicle to take on a six-hour trip to retrieve one of the American bosses the next day. It was under my instruction that he drove that particular armored vehicle on that particular day. Since the Zetas had been following us and casing our company vehicles for months, they had somehow become acquainted with our driving patterns.

They chose that day to take the car. Oh my god, how could this be? I was beyond myself.

What does that phrase really mean? Beyond myself. Literally, I felt like I was watching myself die. The physical feeling of pain was so strong; it felt like it was penetrating with so much force. I could feel my heart beat each and every time. I felt claustrophobic indoors… and had to take several walks outside over the next couple of hours. It was definitely beyond what I could comprehend, emotionally *and* physically. This situation triggered the most uncomfortable, heart-breaking, and harrowing feelings for me. I was in complete anguish.

I have to admit, it felt worse, physically, than when Paolo told me about his sero-conversion. It was up there with my feelings about my cancer and waiting those three horrible days. Only this time, every minute felt like an eternity. I couldn't eat…and I definitely couldn't focus on anything. It was absolutely my worst nightmare realized. When, thirty minutes later, my boss called to tell me that he knew for a fact that Silvestre was alive, still, I could not process what was happening.

In our vehicles at that point in time, we had listen-only microphones installed, so that in case anything like this happened, we could listen in to what was going on. Someone listening heard the Zetas (who at first had no idea they were being tapped) refer to Silvestre in the present tense, which meant for sure he was still alive. Once again, my boss told me he would update me as soon as he had more information and abruptly hung up the phone.

Oddly enough, for this catastrophe, my mother and family were physically present, however, they could not really give the support

I needed because they simply could not grasp the severity of the situation. They had no idea that Silvestre was one of my closest friends and confidants down there. (I wasn't really allowed to speak about the details of my job that much and furthermore, did not want to scare them by speaking of how I had a bodyguard with me, at all times).

As Silvestre was pretty much with me 24/7, he had lived through my near sero-conversion with me, and tons of other fights as well. He had been there for me hundreds of times to listen, mostly by default, but nonetheless he had been there for me always. At this point, I just wanted to know that he was okay. The nausea was worse than ever. I had a splitting headache. I really wanted these physical feelings of pain to stop. To top everything off, I felt completely helpless, the same way I had felt during and after my almost kidnapping. I felt anger. I felt sadness. I felt like every-thing I knew about the world would change, if he were murdered by the cartels. My mind was racing and my heart was sick. I felt sick and disgusted.

I was practically re-living my almost kidnapping, as well as Silvestre's current kidnapping simultaneously. None of my family could fathom what was going on within me. Distracted, I could not even enjoy my beautiful nephew's presence in the room. Again, I told my parents a little bit about what had happened to me my last time in Mexico, however, they had no idea of the grav-ity of either situation. I was trying to protect them from the truth regarding the severity of the dangerous situations in which I con-stantly worked. They were blind... and rightfully so... I really don't think my family could have handled much more. At that point, one week after my sister gave birth to my wonderful and

amazing nephew, her Chron's disease flared up something terrible. Since she was suffering from an intense spasm, my mother
and father were already doting on her incessantly. They just
couldn't really take much more heartache. So I bore this burden
all by myself.

I don't know how I made it through the next three hours. It was
really a cruel joke. My feelings were everywhere and all I could
do was watch sports (which, normally, I hate) and drink water,
which I must have re-filled about five times. At one point, I think
I even got chills.

To be honest, I don't think I would have gone through an
Overwhelmdom phase for quite some time had it not been
for Silvestre's kidnapping. It kick-started my own process and
well done. Thank God. It could have been months or even
years. Dangerous situations like these are definitely not easy
to process.

It was about 1pm when I received the phone call that Silvestre
had been found. He was beaten to within an inch of his life.
Miraculously, fifty miles away from where he had been taken, they
released him about two miles from a major highway. Due to his
bloody and mangled body, he was only able to flag down the third
bus that went by – and only because he stepped right in front of
it. After convincing the bus driver to release him at the nearest
medical center, he was able to borrow someone's cell phone and
contact his security agency. They immediately dispatched police
and my other bodyguard, Manolo, to spend the night with him at
the local hospital.

Manolo was on his way to the hospital. My heart skipped a beat. I took a deep breath in from complete and utter devastation... and relief. My body collapsed, literally and figuratively. I dragged myself to the couch and took a two-hour nap.

When I awoke from my delicious and exhausted nap, all of the feelings were still there, drenched in sweat, through the blood and tears, I honestly felt like I had died and been brought back to life. It would be about eighteen hours before I could personally speak to Silvestre myself, once he was safe and sound in a secure location. He immediately returned to Mexico City, as the security agency felt that he would be safer and better protected from the Zetas, especially given that he was possibly still in danger. After all, they had his full name, address, and company name.

I was told Silvestre wanted to speak with me first thing the following morning. What do you say to someone who has been kidnapped? What not to say? What if he doesn't want to share what happened to him? What if he does want to share? Ugh... It may be that I will have to re-live the entire terrible incident with him. I was perplexed... but at first light, he telephoned me... it was one of those defining moments where I wanted to be the best human being I could be. After all, I was a concerned individual, a leader, a boss, and a friend. Scary!!! I had no idea what to expect, let alone what to say.

To Be Continued...

The Day Manhattan Stood Still

Soon after September 11th, I found I just couldn't handle working at the clothing production place anymore – those Chinese sweatshops were no longer worth my time. It was, I thought, a waste of my talents to be a Production Assistant. 9/11 re-awakened my sense of purpose in all areas of my life. Two to three weeks later, I found a great temp job, which turned into a four-year career in insurance investigations. I know, right? Crazy, but true!

I don't know how I fared in terms of healing from this horrific crime compared to the rest of New Yorkers. I honestly don't know. I mean, Manhattan, normally hustling and bustling with people, urgency, and life, was empty and barren. It was beyond eerie. It was sad. The city was still in **Shock**. Restaurants were closed. Businesses were closed. Yoga was closed. Wow! It would take about one month for the city to get its groove back.

Businesses started to re-open. The sitting shiva period over the course of four weeks had ended and yoga was back up and running again. It's time! The city was definitely wounded for a bit, but we found strength in our fierce nature to endure and rise up again. There's a real reason why New York City is currently building the second tallest building in the world. There is a reason why New York responded with a bang. New York is the financial center of the world and perhaps representative of the world's beating heart. It symbolizes the modern world and humanity. Nothing can keep Manhattan down because nothing can keep humanity down. New York, like the human race, will always avenge and conquer any obstacle in its way. It will always show the world just what hope, thought, success, and courage can achieve.

To be honest, it was the first time that I had felt a deep enough sense of patriotism that I would have joined the marines and actually fought for my country. It would take ten more years before gays could serve openly in the US Army, so that would have been hard for me, since I am used to being beyond open and authentic in my everyday life. Plus, I would have risen in the ranks pretty quickly, I'm sure, just like every other job I have ever had… and heads would have been a-turnin'!

Me, just like New York City, would slowly begin to feel whole again. It was once again a hypersensitive bit of time for me. For one, I would fear low-flying planes for years and years to come. Whatever doesn't kill you will make you stronger. Not only that, it doesn't matter how far down you fall, what matters is how you rise again to beat those and anyone who stands in your way! Freedom and Peace have their price. On September 11th, 2011, we, the United States, remembered that price. I can honestly tell you that, pre-9/11, when traveling on a NYC subway, the crazy or drunken people yelling on the train would control the train. Post 9/11, people would shout, "Shut the hell up already!" as I did on one occasion. And I felt comfortable that at least one other person had my back. Does that make sense? We became less patient with bullshit from the people around us. We also felt more unified as travelers on a subway system, as residents of a city, as citizens of a nation, and even as persons on this Earth. Acts of hatred and destruction always unite the masses. It's just a good old-fashioned fight between good and evil.

Osama Bin Laden definitely thought he was making the statement that even the United States is a vulnerable nation. I doubt that Osama thought that his actions would encourage an even more unified United States and an even bigger cry for freedom and peace in the world. In this battle of good and evil, good always wins… That's just the way it has to be. The good, the moral, the right and the just will always win out over the doubt, the fear, the hate, and the unjust. Also, the vulnerability felt around the world shifted the next generation's perspective of life… meaning we take more pride in finding ourselves, than in finding awesome work. The reverse had worked for the 20th century. No longer.

NYC was **In Overwhelmdom**… it sucked. It was challenging, but we got up, and we haven't stopped bettering ourselves since.

To Be Continued…

A Friend Taken Too Young

So, my trip to Ecuador was planned. I had bought my ticket, and I had survived speaking with both Luli's sister and Luli's mother on multiple occasions. I was flying out three weeks later and it really was the best decision for everyone. They could deal with all of their family and friends on their own time. Then, when I visited down there, we would have our own cathartic reunion of love and friendship.

In the meantime, that weekend, my grandparents' house was just what I needed… to be surrounded by people who love and cherish me to the highest degree. I lived about three hundred miles away from my family. I thought that was far enough to be a good solid distance, but close enough to be able to get in the car and be home within about five to six hours. That worked for me. Still, with difficult and challenging situations, it felt too far.

It was about ten days after I heard the news of Luli's death that my **Mock-cceptance** stopped abruptly and I went into full-blast **Overwhelmdom** mode. I remember it was a sunny Saturday morning. There was nothing special happening that day or that weekend for that matter. I know that I had awoken very aware of my feelings, sounds, traffic, that which puts the *life* into life. I thought I was just having one of my "feeling" days. I called them "feeling" days because every two to three months, I would have a couple of days when my emotions were completely on my sleeve, I was a little more sensitive, and any little thing could make me tear up or make me feel very warm and fuzzy. I don't really have those days anymore. As I have been called an "empath", I used to take on other people's emotions and feelings. I have now learned to set boundaries in all aspects of my life... and I'm still in the process of doing just that – even today.

Anyway... that sunny Saturday, ten days after Luli had passed away, my partner had a morning rendez-vous with someone, and either I wasn't invited, or I didn't feel like going. When I am **In Overwhelmdom**, I tend to stay close to home and NOT put myself in any major social situations (unless necessary) where I'm going to have to be Seth. Being Seth, by the way, is not always easy. People easily recognize and remember me because I'm always smiling on the outside and inside, always being positive, always warm and honest, etc.... when I'm in one of these moods, it's the last thing I want to do... be more of Seth! Everyone has sad days or difficult days. If I can't be the dependably cheerful young man people are expecting of me, I retreat as much as possible so as to remain constant with people. If I can't be sincerely cheerful, I'd rather not be there at all!

So, my boyfriend was gone and I woke up very late. I walked several blocks North for some reason, as I remember exactly where I was when the slew of emotions hit me - at the 24/7 deli/store. Can you believe that I lived by this deli/store for over two years, and I could never remember the name of it? Not even now. I went in there probably two to three times per week, but still could never for the life of me remember the name of the store. It's really not important for this story, and I guess it wasn't important to my life and that's why I didn't memorize it! I was walking back from wherever I was, when I felt this incredible and overwhelming feeling of heaviness.

I thought I was going to throw up. When I made it home, the tears started flowing. It took me all of five milliseconds to pinpoint the exact reason: Luli's passing. It became crystal clear because the moment the thought passed through my mind, I started bawling uncontrollably. I felt anger for the first time about Luli's death. It is rare for me that emotions will overwhelm my heart this much and I will be clueless as to what their purpose is. In those instances, I usually take what I like to call an emotional inventory of what has been going on.

I guess I wasn't going to throw up after all. Nope, just a good cry. In fact, it hit me so hard, that it knocked the wind right out of me, and I couldn't quite make it to the bathtub (I like to cry in showers). Oddly enough, my body was mid-way between the master bedroom and the master bath. It was a quaint place for a good sob... and I mean, I was sobbing.

Luli had lived in New Jersey the previous year, on and off for nine months and the guilt of not seeing her more shined through right away. I was sad. I was nauseated. I would never see this young lady again. She was twenty-six when she died. The details of her death at this point were still quite the mystery to me. I felt anger! Angry at God, and angry at the universe. Why her? Why would the world take away such an amazing creature on this Earth?

The year before she had also been crowned "Miss Ecuador, New York City"... I know it's a little cheesy, but it was the New York City Miss Ecuador pageant. She was incredibly beautiful... and I was there when she won. Even though it was way out in Jackson Heights, Queens, it counted for us. (If you have lived in New York, you know what a schlep that is!) We were all elated and full of laughter afterwards for the sheer madness and craziness of it all. We three, Majo, Luli, and myself had lived through quite a few disasters, triumphs, and successes. When Luli was around, the world felt a little bit more palatable.

I sat there on the floor for about twenty minutes, crying my heart out, until my boyfriend came home. I thought it would be a little dramatic for him to find me on the floor, so I thought I would move and cry on the toilet, like most men when they seek privacy to cry. Turns out, both of my feet were asleep and I wasn't going anywhere. Turning the corner to the bathroom, he was extremely concerned first about whether I had fallen or not. All I could muster between my sobbing inhales and exhales that Luli was dead. He knew then that this was the ugly cry. This was the cry I had been waiting for... rather we had been waiting for. He picked me up, positioned me on the bed, and caressed me for about fifteen more minutes while I finished crying and then started talking about the good old times with Luli. The guilt rose again and subsided... the anger rose again, then subsided, then the sadness arose... and stayed within me for about two more weeks.

Life seemed a bit slower, and a bit more serious. I was getting into yoga at that point, which was the perfect outlet for me. It's about now that I should tell you that in the span of two to three years, I lost four close friends. Max, seventeen, the son of a very influential mentor of mine, drowned in the icy waters off the New York City islands in a terrible boating incident. Santiago, twenty-five, a close friend of my boyfriend and mine, died of a brain tumor. He lived six years after being told by the head of Memorial Sloan-Kettering Cancer Center neurological division that he would die within a few months. Go Santiago!!! He was a character. Luli, twenty-six, passed away from a brain hemorrhage, as I would later find out. Lastly, Vinny, sixty-five, died from AIDS, after having lived for over twenty years as HIV+. It was a crazy couple of years… and I did a LOT of work on death and resolution. Luli was my closest friend and confidant, which is why I am focusing on her in this book, but each of these people touched me equally during his or her short span of life. They were all magical in their own way.

Oi! The challenges! It was a bitter ride through an intense world. New York City sometimes can burn you out. It is so full to the brim of success, intense success, and money, and life… that it can completely over-stimulate you. One must know how to navigate the city, even when your chips are down or your chips feel down. What happened next will amaze you… talk about magical…

To Be Continued…

5 THINGS TO REMEMBER WHEN IN OVERWHELMDOM

1.   Trust the Process. Acknowledge the Emotions and the Craziness.

Trust in your body and mind's way of healing. Trust that you are exactly where you need to be. Trust that this too shall pass. Know that everything you are feeling is normal and part of the journey. If you feel numb, be numb. If you are hurt, feel the pain. If you feel vulnerable, be vulnerable! (I know it's hard for everyone, and I mean everyone!) Cry, if you need to. You will get through this. You will. If you haven't read the book, Today, I Feel Silly *by Jamie Lee Curtis, then you are missing out! It is one of my absolute favorites.*

2.   Get Comfortable.

Get your favorite blanket, your cozy clothes, and your stuffed animals or delicious pets. Take-out menus? Make sure all of your take-out menus are in alphabetical order or organized by food type! (A quick shout out to my fellow O.C.D. peeps!) Record as many TV shows as possible to last 3-5 weeks. Comedies, Dramas, and movies all have an amazing ability to take us away to Hollywood-land or Bollywood-land. Be carried away, you could probably use the distraction. Lastly, treat yourself as warmly and kindly as you treat your pets.

3.   When One Door Closes, A New One Opens.

Poor endings = fun new beginnings. Unfortunately, everything must come to an end, right? And with every finality there comes an amazing and awe-bound opportunity. The best thing ever could be waiting on the other side of the new door.

4.   *Testing Your Patience.*

Be prepared for the universe to test your patience and throw you little curveballs. Sometimes it might feel like the universe (God, the gods, fate, providence - whatever is your pleasure) is kicking you while you're down. For example, when boarding a plane in Mexico, after running from one terminal to another... with minutes left... and for some odd reason, there is an out-of-the-ordinary problem with your status. Ugh. These moments remind us that it could always be worse.

5.   *Feel Your Feelings.*

If you want to just shrivel up and die... congratulations! You are now human. You are lucky to be alive and, remember, feelings and emotions are a lot like farts... they come and go, sometimes they are loud and obnoxious, sometimes they are short and to the point. Sometimes they are silent and peaceful, and other times they are silent and deadly.

IN OVERWHELMDOM - Conclusion:

"Ugh!" - **In Overwhelmdom** is the culmination of personal and unique individual emotions. It is a hypersensitivity to all that goes on around you. Don't be surprised if you really have no patience to listen to anyone else's drama… or just the reverse - I wouldn't be surprised if all you want to do is listen to other people's drama. It is the part where the real work is about to begin and your mind, body, and soul are preparing you for the task at hand – healing. It is not pretty. The ugly cry will be a part of this phase. Always. Just accept it.

Here is a laundry list of emotions you might feel: Rage, Hurt, Fear, Sadness, Elation, Pain, Anguish, Exhaustion, Indifference, Discomfort, Horror, Terror, Love, Hate, Nervousness, Embarrassment, and always on the Verge of Tears (for no reason). The list goes on and on. There is no way around it. Your emotions are all over the place… and as they are arbitrary and blow with the wind, there is no use in fighting them. Acknowledge that you are a little emotional right now and there is absolutely nothing wrong with that. You cannot really fix it either, it's just a matter of time, patience, and awareness.

Handling all of these emotions directly depends on your "forma de ser" or "way of being," (a beautiful concept frequently used in Spanish). Your "way of being" is a direct result of that which you have endured throughout your life, starting with the formative years passing through the bumpy and angsty teenage years, the taunting twenties, the serious thirties, the settled forties, and so on. The result of all your experiences and all your healing is your "forma de ser"; and based upon this, you will either be overtaken by the anger, sadness, and depression, or acknowledge your emotions, and ride the ever-changing wave of emotion with grace.

Take your entire experiential history, the good, the bad, the beautiful, and the ugly, and see just how well you acclimate to life currently. How well you handle life and all its curve balls determines how happy your life is! Work through your past. Forgive others. Take the higher road. Be the better person, share the love, and always express more love!

If you have managed to forgive and take the higher road from time to time, that's awesome! You are **Learning**. This shows an incredible amount of confidence, inner-strength, and knowing. It's better to be happy than to win, right? Sometimes it's better to honor and respect your relationship, than to indulge the ugly ego… and possibly lose everything. If you haven't managed to forgive once in a while or take the higher road, try it. No judgments. It's extremely difficult in the moment but it eventually opens you to more joy and pride.

So, choose to ride the poignant emotions or choose to let them reign over you. The choice is again yours. Either way, you will feel some intense emotions. Don't be afraid. You will overcome this just like you have overcome all of those other obstacles in your past. It will be tough. It will be a challenge. It can also be invigorating and exciting. Who knows what emotion will come out next? Don't be too hard on yourself either! Most of us, myself included, have the tendency to be very hard on our own selves. Be easy on yourself. Let the feelings come and go. As quickly as they arrive, let them go. As intense as they are, don't let them get the best of you. All of these extreme feelings will run their course and then pass. It is natural to feel all of these emotions passionately.

You can't escape **Overwhelmdom**, no matter how much it hurts to feel emotions or how much it sucks to relish in an emotional rollercoaster. It is the natural, incredible process of healing. Watch yourself next time tragedy strikes. Remember, as I'm always saying, in life, pain is inevitable, but suffering is optional.

After you conquer your individual robust range of emotions, you can then proceed to an easier and more relaxed Smile From the Inside way of living. I never said this process was easy. It can chill you to the bone, if you let it. I believe some people get stuck in this part of the process and therefore might never move forward on the journey to healing. It's never too late to move forward along in the S.M.I.L.E. process.

In Overwhelmdom, we ride the emotional superhighway of our life. This is the part of the yoga class where you are sweating profusely, breathing for your life, and you really just don't think you can hold the pose for another FOUR breaths. It's just not gonna happen. If you stick with it, however, you will feel accomplished, proud, and a huge sense of empowerment.

Overwhelmdom is where all of the warm-ups (**Shock**) and the conditioning (**Mock-cceptance**) finally pay off. It is the key step to the overall adjustment that is imminently going to happen within your life. Thus, it's the third important step we all must conquer to live a more balanced and more centered Smile From The Inside life.

LEARNING

STAGE FOUR: LEARNING.
Learning
noun

1. Any lasting change in behavior, resulting from experience, especially conditioning.

2. The act or process of acquiring knowledge or skill, or knowledge gained by study.[10]

---

10   Colman, Andrew M, Oxford Dictionary of Psychology. Oxford University Press, 2009.

Expressed Feeling = "Ohhh... Wow!"

Learning. Here's what I think: this is where you surrender yourself to the way things are, right now, in the present. This is the hardest part of the journey, because it is not about taking control of the situation. It is about understanding how to "be" with the situation. **Learning** stage is about figuring out how to "live" with the situation and how to "move forward," knowing what you know now. Does it sound easy? It's definitely *not* easy at all. In fact, this is where you put your big pants on and handle what needs to be handled and resolve what needs to be resolved! Hence, **"Ohhh... Wow!"**

I believe that with surrender to any situation inevitably comes fear. Admitting that we are not in control of the circumstances of the traumatic event can be scary. Acknowledging that a change is in order and enacting that change can also be fearful at first. The key to **Learning** is letting things be and knowing that everything will be all right someday very soon. It is not such a bad thing. Sometimes knowing that everything will change can work in your favor.

Just a word about control. I used to think it was necessary to be in control; perhaps that was the obsessive-compulsive side of me. Thanks, Mom and Dad! (My parents are a little O.C.D.). I have recently learned that I do not have to hold it all together, all the time. Believe me, sometimes it is just too much pressure. **Learning** to release the urge to hold it all together liberated me from the constraints of complete control. This was probably one of the biggest lessons I have learned in my life. It feels just like the song "I Can See Clearly Now"... *I can see clearly now, the rain is gone.*

I can see clearly now, the rain is gone -
I can see all obstacles in my way.
Gone are the dark clouds that had me blind.
It's gonna be a bright, bright, bright, bright
Sunshiny day.

I think I can make it now, the pain is gone -
All of the bad feelings have disappeared.
Here is the rainbow I've been praying for.
Look all around, there's nothing but blue skies.
Look straight ahead, nothing but blue skies!

-Johnny Nash, 1972

I noticed while working in Mexico that Mexicans have mastered the concept of surrender. There are so many problems all the time! They live in a constant state of accepting their current surroundings. I argue, however, that instead of continuing to accept the status quo, you choose to start creating a different and better life. Choose to begin again, designing and creating a new and better existence. Everything in life begins with a choice. That means that in every moment we can make a new choice or we can choose the same old, same old. At any given second, we can choose a new approach, something unique to say, or something different to do. Powerful concept, isn't it?

Learning to surrender is where you take off the earrings and pull back the sista' scrunchy, and get ready to play dirty. Get ready to roll with the punches! And you better be ready to see the reality for what it is and move forward! The present can be scary. The present can be daunting. **Learning** is a vulnerable place. **Learning** is an acute and invasive honesty. And, honesty, as we all know, is not easy... Living in reality can be full of emotions and full of awkward moments. It won't always be comfortable and it won't always be a bowl of cherries. Keep the chocolate and/or the alcohol close! Now would be a great time to plan some fun things.

Just know that, as everything else does, this initial jolt of awkwardness and discomfort will subside... as this surrender sinks in to your quotidian practices. Develop some new routines. Create your life as you want it. Create your day as you want to. In this stage, I would suggest you start reading some "New Age/Self-Help" books. They might be able to offer some deeper thoughts and further insights into your experiences. Have fun!

If **Shock** warms up the mind and body, **Mock-cceptance** conditions the mental and physical you, and **In Overwhelmdom** ignites every emotion possible, pushing you to your limits, then **Learning** allows you the opportunity to physiologically and psychologically process the event that just occurred in your world. In the yoga world, arm balances are tough! **Learning** to fall, laugh, and try, try again becomes important to mastering the pose. Through my stories, you will see how **Learning** paves the way for the last step in the S.M.I.L.E. Method, **Embrace**, which is the true healing. With the surrender associated with **Learning** from your mistakes, your actions, and your behaviors, you will feel empowered and motivated, two more concepts essential to the Smile From The Inside experience.

Um... You Lost Me At Cancer

After the overwhelming feelings subsided and road rage was a quick and distant memory, I started to gather myself together. I started to sing again. I started to feel a more regular range of emotions. I started to review what had happened to me over the past 6-8 weeks. It was quite the run. It was quite the experience. It was probably one of the scariest things that had ever happened to me, other than the aforementioned almost kidnapping or the day I was held at gun-point by the Colombian guerrillas in 1998.

It was time to reflect. I was still sad. Don't mistake what I'm saying, Sadness is a by-product and natural progression of healing. As my therapist asks, what's negative about feeling sad? Absolutely nothing! Reflection is usually a non-partial way of looking back at an event, devoid of emotions, and truly seeing, hearing, or **Learning**, reminding us of what I call life lessons. These life lessons are the gifts of trials and tribulations. They are the gifts that arise from pain and sadness. They prevent us from perhaps making the same mistakes yet again and usually keep us humble. We are forever **Learning** and forever evolving beings. It was time to see just exactly what I had learned from this terrific and daunting experience.

Most of my **Learning** precipitated when I was completing a cancer survivor questionnaire. It was the Cancer Center's brilliant attempt to find out how they can provide better and better care, both physically, emotionally, and medically speaking. The one question that struck a deep chord was, "If you could tell someone who has just been diagnosed with cancer some things to keep in mind and expect, what would they be?" At first, I really had to think about this question. It was an amazing question and I felt that my answer might truly help an individual the next time around. No one should have to deal with this in his or her lifetime, yet so many do. I knew that my answer could make a huge difference in at least one person's life, if not many. For this reason, I find it to be incredibly apropos to share with you here (the **Learning** section) a couple of the suggestions I wrote down that particular day, in greater detail. I believe these ideas are important for everyone to know regarding the sharing *any* type of news, really.

Each person will react differently - guaranteed. Your mother will react differently than your father. One good friend will react differently from your other BFFs. It is important to refrain from passing judgment on anyone. Sad news can be challenging to hear for the best of times, let alone for the majority of the world out there. Your news could influence them slightly. Don't be surprised if some friends politely and quietly remove themselves from you (which happened to me during my time of need). I know, it sounds a bit heartless, but some people just cannot deal with additional distressing news on top of whatever else is going on in their lives.

At first, truth be told, I was a bit disappointed in my own friends who quietly removed themselves, however, once they finally did reach out, they expressed genuine interest and concern. After a while, I realized that it was they who had the issues. Their distance had very little to do with me. You don't know if someone has lost a mother or father or close grandparent to cancer, AIDS, etc. We really don't ever know why people make some of their interesting choices. A few years later, in fact, I did mention it to one of my friends, who in his fabulous way proceeded to tell me,

"Oh, honey, you know I don't do Death, Dying, or Cancer. It's all just too sad. Didn't I come back right after your situation was ending?" Hilarious!

Choose not to hold on to any resentments or disappointments. Instead, as in my case, we now see each other a few times per year, and that's fine and dandy. Life has a strange way of coming around. Now, unfortunately, my friend is a bit sick and going through something... and I will NOT distance myself at all. Nope, instead, I am seeing him with more and more frequency. No questions asked. No requests from his part. It's all my choice. Just because he doesn't do death, dying, or cancer, does not mean that I don't do it!

Something else everyone should know: It just might be the case that you will need to comfort your friends and family first. This sounds a bit odd, I know, but, it is the truth. Prior to your family taking care of you, they will need some support from you. This happened with several of my relationships, as well as with my family. My family tends to deal with things immediately and process quickly. Come on, we're Jews, we are used to grief and sadness, right? (Some day, I would like to break that old-fashioned stereotype).

Yes, my family needed me to be the strong one for the first two weeks, while each one of them dealt with my cancer news. They needed time to adjust to the upsetting information. I had to be brave, confident, and hopeful for them – even though once we got off the phone, I felt I didn't have any more for myself. After the first two weeks, my family came around quickly and positively. My sister, my aunt, and my parents were there for me 100%... and after two weeks of being strong, brave, and hopeful, I needed to let someone else take the reins and allow someone else to take care of me. It was literally perfect timing, 'cause I felt at that point, I had nothing else to give or share.

Next, the support and encouragement around you is so bloody important. Apart from my family, without having support from my friends, I could not have physically made it through those days. One of my BFFs took me to the hospital and home, and my roommates helped me dress and shower (God bless those three individuals). As I told you earlier, my co-workers came to visit me… they are forever in my thoughts as well. I don't think people realize quite how much visits have a tremendous impact on the patient, not only on the patient's current status, but also a visit gives you a special gold star forever more. Take my word for it! People tend to remember those that came to visit them either in the hospital or their couch, even when they are pumped full of Dilaudid or Vicodin.

Next piece of friendly advice: When you are in your own stuff, set boundaries for the people around you. You give them an inch for their miseries, and they'll take advantage of the mile. It's not often that we feel at our wit's end emotionally. During times of extreme emotion or reflection, it is especially okay to set boundaries with people. I actually told people several times that I don't really want to talk about their stuff… nor my own stuff, I'd rather talk about superficial items like what's in the latest issue of U.S. Weekly.

It is heavy and burdensome dealing with your own illness comprehension or deathly questions, so listening to someone else's life/problems can definitely be beyond overwhelming. Be straight with your friends. Be honest with your family.

They will understand. I promise you they will understand. They will also appreciate it because it means that you care enough about them to want to hear about their stuff, just not now. Set those boundaries. It helps. Sometimes, all I did was want my friends to come over, order pizza, watch movies, then go home. Those moments were priceless to me and were much needed. Just being in the presence of those who love you gives hope, makes me feel part of the world, and ALIVE. Never underestimate the magical and healing power of just spending time with a good friend.

Lastly, I want everyone to know that **Life can be pretty hairy sometimes...** Life can be ugly. Life can be horrendous and taxing. It is in moments of daunting nature, that we, as humans, experience without doubt that we either have everything we need to survive or we do NOT.

Spiritually speaking, we have everything that we need in life. All of our needs are met. Our inner-strength is unlimited and will always be tested by everyone and everything around us. We have the capability and the opportunity to rise above anything, to be anything, and to do anything and everything. For most of us, getting up in the morning is a challenge. For others of us, from the moment we wake up in the morning, we are ready to challenge whatever is coming our way.

It is in the darkest moments of human existence that our light can and will shine the brightest. We can discover that darkness is only temporary and that the light within us burns infinitely and will forever be available to us... long after our last physical dying breath. It is the seed of our soul and the life force, which penetrates and bursts through us, around us.

Cancer has taught me to live more in the moment. I am up in the air about whether my cancer was a result of the twelve to fourteen hours I spent outside in sunny New England from June to September without sunscreen, or a side-effect of having been really depressed the entire previous year due to my horrific breakup with J. I think it was a bit of both issues that caused the skin cancer to occur. I mean, when J. broke it off with me, and I promptly moved across the ocean to L.A., I was "depressed" for months and months. I was not clinically depressed, but I was very, very sad... to the point where I stopped taking on life coaching clients as well as stopped doing yoga. (That's saying a lot because I am a Yogi through and through - I had practiced yoga three to four times per week for about five years).

Does it really matter what caused it? No. I just wanted to point out there is a real connection between the mind and the body, a very real connection, that I will never doubt again after my situation. In the name of **Learning**, I was still trying to figure out what cancer had to offer me on my path. I thought I was already compassionate and humble enough. Perhaps I needed to be reminded of how precious life is and how little time we have on this Earth as physical beings, right? It would take me a while longer to finally accept then **Embrace** this whole cancer thing as a part of my incredible life.

Here's a reminder, though, to all surviving cancer patients. It could always be worse. I'm going to tell you a little story - a little story of a love affair, between a middle-aged lesbian cancer survivor, Linda, and a little gay man, me. From the very first moment I laid eyes on Linda, I couldn't help but be in love. Linda owned a pottery shop here in Los Angeles, and I took Paolo to learn how to "throw". I know now, that I gained a great deal more than pottery from this woman with whom I had only shared two conversations prior to falling in love. She was a force. She exuded light and love with everything she did. Being with her, I felt important and super, super special. The first time I met Linda, we clicked from the get-go and I was touched by her. She taught us the amazing poetic dance of "throwing" clay... and I yielded some sort of a shape consistent with a dog bowl. Pottery is not as easy at it looks, at least not for me.

Two weeks later, she telephoned to let me know that our pots were ready for pick up. We talked for a few minutes on the phone, and it was my full intention to collect them. I didn't go pick them up. Four weeks later, she telephoned me to inform me that our pots were still ready for pick up. That time, we spoke for about ten minutes about random things. I still didn't go pick them up. Nope, I didn't go pick them up for another two months after that.

It was at the height of the sero-conversion part of my life, so I was in quite the daze. When I walked in to the pottery studio, I noticed that she was a bit frail. I didn't want to be rude and ask. Usually, I can sense these types of things from people. About the same time I noticed her ailing health, she asked if something was wrong with me. Linda actually walked me outside and allowed me to cry on her shoulder for about ten minutes. After, she relayed to me that she had been going through chemo for her second type of cancer. I was like, what? Your *second* type of cancer? Wow... she had listened to me go on and on for ten minutes about my boyfriend who had recently sero-converted, and she was the one that could possibly be dying... did I ever feel embarrassed.

To Be Continued...

I Thought We Were Monogamous!

Literally, Learning is about discovery, self-discovery, investigation, analysis, and lots and lots of emotions. More precisely it is **Learning** to surrender to the present situation - to the tragic element of events. I left off where Paolo and I were making lists of people to tell, including my parents. Up until that point, I was more focused on the present and future of how our lives would change, but I never looked at exactly *how* this all had happened.

After completing our lists, one by one, we would either invite them over to the house for drinks and apps, something that us gays do very well. After we've all had one drink, it was then time to share our latest news. Paolo would always start the conversation. He was always joking around with friends, so people never knew at first if he was serious or just trying to pull their leg. They would look to me and when my face was deadpan serious, it immediately became clear that he was not doing his usual rouse. Nope. This time he was dead serious.

Sharing this type of information with people is not like sharing that you are pregnant. It's not like sharing any type of good news. It's not exactly like you are telling people you have cancer, but it is emotionally taxing to share and it is uncomfortable and awkward for all parties involved. I am glad I had researched the updated facts on POZ-living, because many things had changed since I first learned about it in school fourteen years before.

Sometimes the support and encouragement was immediate and overflowing while other times the individual would be in **Shock**. Constant questions would be... what does that mean? Really, are you serious? You see, people can only process information so fast and sometimes this type of health/death information enters the mind one sentence at a time. No judgments. Another question asked was what about Seth? Yeah. What about me? I mean, if he contracted it, and we were actively practicing unsafe sex with each other, how could I NOT have contracted it. We were as perplexed then as I am now. We'll return to that thought in a bit.

Did you know that there is a medical gene mutation known as CCR5-Delta 32, which exists in ten percent of white people, usually with European or North European decent? Apparently, these are the only known individuals to have any type of natural selection immunity to the HIV. Since we didn't know that he was infected, we continued having unprotected sex perhaps two to three times after he had potentially contracted it.

Unbelievably, and much to my amazement, no one would ask, well how did you contract it? I guess that is considered rude or at least no one asked me that in front of Paolo. Which brings me to my next point... how the hell did he contract it? I sure wanted to know that. Thank God we were in couple's counseling when this all came about because I probably would have gone nuts. Would you believe me if I told you, it took about three months to figure out how *most likely* he had contracted the disease? I mean, let's be honest. I'm pretty sure he was not an IV drug user, there were no recent hospitalizations or blood transfusions, and apparently, he had NEVER cheated on me. In fact, to this day, he contends that he NEVER cheated on me, which is a boldface lie as certain persons have told me they fooled around with him during the time we were together. That's not so surprising to me. I guess it isn't that impor- tant in the grand scheme of things, but for me, the continued lying, uncertainty, and dishonesty became more and more important, and it ultimately led to the destruction and downfall of our relationship.

When we asked ourselves the question of how he contracted it, we also had to tell the third person, with whom we recently (the month prior) had had a three-way. Poor kid was devastated. I had convinced myself a hundred percent that he was the one who had brought this into our lives. Remember, folks, denial - not just ignorance - is bliss. After scaring the poor kid to death, it turns out that he was HIV negative, like me. That took one whole week - one week of my actually believing that my boyfriend had always been faithful to me. One week of me actually feeling that Paolo would have definitely come clean if he had been unfaithful. But, he didn't! For some reason, he couldn't. And I was the schmuck. I was the clueless boyfriend who was dumb enough to think better of him.

I gave him multiple occasions where he could have easily confessed to me if he had, in fact, slept with someone else. At that point, anything probably would have been better than not knowing how exactly he had been exposed. IT had to have been someone who either didn't know he was POZ or he knew and didn't say anything. After the poor kid came clean as negative, my senses were shot and I was *stunned*. It then had to be Paolo who contracted the HIV virus from someone OUTSIDE of the relationship. Even at such a juncture, he continued to deny the inevitable truth of the situation.

It was yours truly who finally shed some light onto this conundrum. I vaguely remember one night that happened the month prior, July. We were out, I was tired and went home early. If I am being honest, which I should be, it is more likely that he was being obnoxious and I couldn't handle it yet again. (That's what you get when you pick bad boys and want to heal them from their deepest and darkest sorrows and experiences). At about 1:35am, I received a phone call from Paolo. Since we were big texters, I knew immediately there might be something wrong. It was garbled and he kept saying, "Please help. Please help! Get 'em off me! Don't touch me." I was horrified.

In our relationship, I was definitely used to crazy and rare experiences and thought I was prepared for anything. I racked my brain trying to figure out what to do... so, finally, I asked him where he was? It took him about thirty seconds to comprehend exactly what I was asking... he said, I don't know, close to the house... grass. Aha! I knew where he had been all night, as we had been texting periodically, and I knew it had to be between the bar and our home, which was about five blocks. And I know of only one place where there was grass. I told him to hang on and I would be right there. Like a bat out of hell, I drove the car literally into the other lane of traffic... as I knew that to be the fastest way to arrive at the grassy knoll without crashing into a median. I saw Paolo, on the ground, with a few people around him.

Once I approached him, he looked horrible, disheveled, and completely out of sorts. He was kicking the people that were apparently helping him up. They ran over to me and asked are you this "Babeee" he keeps crying for... to which I responded, yes. (It was an inside pet name). Wow! They told me they had found him with his pants down and beaten up. They also told me that he was extremely aggressive and kept kicking everyone who tried to help him to his feet. It took three of us about ten minutes to get him into the back seat of the car. Paolo calmed down a little when he realized it was me.

Paolo proceeded to pass out in the back of the car. Great! How was I going to get him up one flight of stairs and into bed safely? Let's just say that after about thirty minutes of him literally kicking and screaming at us to get off of him and to stay away from him, a neighbor and I managed to get him into bed, where I cleaned his face and put him in new clothes. It was such a terrible experience, I'm not surprised I had even forgotten about it... but I probably stored the event in one of the far reaches of my mind as just another crazy day in my life. The next day, Paolo discovered that two hundred dollars worth of cash was stolen from his wallet, and he was convinced he was robbed right before he passed out on the grass.

When I proceeded to do my due diligence and calculations of when and where he would have been exposed to the HIV virus in order for his numbers to be where they were three to four weeks later, it, at first, dawned on me that more might have happened to him that evening. Poor thing, I thought. When I gently brought this up in one therapy session, he convinced himself that that was the case and that he may have, in fact, been victimized and robbed all at the same time. I, on the other hand, wasn't so convinced. In fact, from that moment on, I started to distance myself from him, physically, emotionally, and in every way possible.

I'm not proud to say it, but this distance ultimately led to my spontaneous infidelities over the course of one week when he was away for work in November. Two weeks after my week of indiscretions, I came clean. In his culture, it is perfectly okay for men to cheat on their women, but quite a different reaction occurs when the reverse happens. He took this as a personal affront against him. I should have left him then, but there was this silly ethical and moral voice - or sadomasochistic side of me - that wanted to honor my pledge to stick with him through this until the end. I am a man of my word, because let's face it; if you have nothing else, you always have your word, which is your honor.

For me, in this situation, I found the truth. I found the missing piece for me to cope with this situation, and it led to the inevitable end. See, I learned that I would never believe him about that unfortunate night and I could never trust him and, for me, that is one of the most important ground values needed to have a solid and happy relationship. Nope, for me the problem was not the HIV. I could easily continue to live with two separate worlds i.e. toothbrushes, razors, etc. I couldn't, however, live with the uncertainty, the deceit, the lies, and the unwilling attitude to explore beyond that one unfortunate night. To be honest, I mostly believed him about what could have perhaps happened that night and I truly am sorry if that, in fact, happened to him. I just couldn't believe it fully. I could not accept that. Even before the sero-conversion, in the relationship, I often felt like I was a poor individual caught in a hundred mile-per-hour wind storm, fighting against those wind currents and it was only getting stronger and the odds of surviving were only growing weaker and weaker.

At last, I surrendered to the fact that I would probably never know the truth about how Paolo contracted the HIV virus. At the end of the day, it really bothered me... too much so, in fact. It became clear to me that this was perhaps not the right relationship for me, regardless of whether or not he had HIV, cancer, or any life-threatening or life-compromising disease. I valued myself too much and I loved myself too much. However, all that being said, I still continued in the relationship, as unhappy as I was because of my word and promise to him.

We were diagnosed in August and the quest for the truth took us through to late October. All that time I lived without answers, and without any hope of a changed future. I mean, think about it, our whole future had changed. We couldn't even mention children anymore; he desperately wanted children from his bloodline. I did lots of research on this... and uncovered there were new studies reporting that he could possibly have his own children in the very near future. But he couldn't hear that either.

I don't pretend to know what he was going through, but I feel like I had a damn good idea. It was terrible, horrible, and beyond what any person should have to deal with in the course of a lifetime. Kudos to him (and all other POZ peeps) for getting up every morning strong, happy, and proud. Seriously. Amongst all of the crazy and overwhelming emotions we had experienced, I stretched and flexed to the limits of craziness for him. I was there for him constantly and consistently, until I could not be with *him* anymore. I had definitely surrendered to our changed existence and our changed relationship. In my heart of hearts, I thought that perhaps it would inspire him and encourage him to disengage from certain poor behavioral patterns that I thought were destructive. Alas, it did not. And, alas, no matter how much you may want to change someone, you cannot change anyone. And I am a firm believer that you only get the honored task of accepting your partner as 100% who they are. I just could *not* accept *all* of him. It was his inability to love, honor, and respect me as much as I needed, and the fact that I could never really trust him after the sero-conversion. Either way, it was devastating to the both of us.

So, you know what's coming, right? It took me about three months even after coming clean about my indiscretions to finally make the decision to end our two-year relationship…

To Be Continued…

Un Secuestro en México – A Kidnapping in Mexico

We left off where I was waiting to speak with Silvestre after his Express Kidnapping. I barely slept that night. He emailed me from his personal email address saying he desperately wanted to speak with me and that he would call me around 10am. When I received the phone call, I just kind of stared blankly at my cell phone, taking a few final breaths before I had to coach this poor person who had just been kidnapped, and listen to his story, console him, then probably say goodbye to him for a while. I started to get very nervous and shake.

Finally, I picked up. It was a ghost of a voice. A usually strong and confident man now had the voice of a scared schoolboy who had just been berated by his teacher in front of the rest of the class. Yes, we've all been there. Silvestre was quiet and reserved. Note: Silvestre was never quiet and reserved. I relayed how relieved I was to hear his voice and that he was kept alive. I proceeded to ask him how he was doing, if he had told his mom or if he was ever going to tell his mother? Of course, he replied, never. I told him that I would respect his privacy and if he wanted to share details with me, that was fine, but otherwise, I was just happy that he was alive and speaking to me on the phone at the very moment.

He really wanted to tell me the story, so he took a big breathe and divulged the entire story to me. He was basically dragged out of the vehicle, blindfolded and gagged, and then beaten almost to death. They miraculously let him go about a hundred kilometers away from where they had stolen the vehicle… and they also returned his bag and computer to him. He was completely bloody and had to flag down a few buses before one of them finally pulled over to the side to pick him up, because he gave the bus no other alternative. With his bloody self, he stood right in front of the bus to ensure that it had to stop. It was an absolutely horrific story.

Usually when I speak to people on the phone at home, I pace around the house aimlessly but with a focused purpose. For this conversation, I actually had to sit down outside on my sister's porch. I had to remind myself to breathe.

When he finished his shocking story, which of course I interrupted various times to get a more vivid picture, I was stunned. It takes a great deal for anyone to stun me to the point of verbal annihilation. I didn't want too much time to go by before I said anything, so I spoke from the heart. I told him that I loved him (for the very first time), that no one should ever have to experience anything like that, and that since he was definitely a little unhappy being out on our properties, in the middle of nowhere, so far away from his family, from women, and civilization, he could look on the bright side - now he could go home, get girls, and return to civilization, clubs, etc. He laughed and told me how much he truly is going to miss not just the job, but me. It was very, very sweet. Think about it, I had probably spent the majority of my waking hours with this guy for almost two years.

He was definitely a very good friend. Remember, Silvestre was there *all* the time. He even drove me back to the airport the day I found out that Paolo had contracted HIV. It's a long ride, and he heard my phone calls, my crying, the whole damn thing...

I stayed on the phone with him for the better part of an hour, listened to him, consoled him, teased him, knowing that this was probably going to be the last time I would speak to him for quite a while because it would not be safe for me or him to continue communication for a bit. I was pretty sad. In fact, I was very, very sad. It was as if my BFF was leaving forever. My rock. My staple. My friend. I reminded him that everything happens for a reason and that his leaving was probably for the best. I know he did enjoy his lifestyle with us, but he had to move on to bigger and better things. When we hung up the phone, one of the last things he said to me was, "I'll never forget you and I love you too, man!" It put such a smile on my face. I knew that he would have a difficult time over the next few weeks, or months, but I *knew* he would survive this and go on to do incredible and unbelievable things. Silvestre is an amazing individual who only deserves happiness and lots and lots of girls.

Later that day, my boss contacted me to say that it was time we start talking about if I was ever going to return to Mexico. He wanted me to seriously consider all the pros and cons. My boss was a true gentleman about the whole situation, even suggesting that I didn't have to think about it long. I told him that I would probably never be stepping foot in Mexico ever again, so that would make it pretty difficult for me to continue with my role... that I ADORED and LOVED so much. He iterated that he would try to find me something else within the company, and we then started to work out a three-month transition plan. I'll never forget one of the last things he said to me, "I'm proud of you, Seth. I never thought you were going to last two years, given the violence that besieged Mexico during that period of time." I was **Shock**ed and surprised.

When my boss left with me those parting words was when I started to surrender to the **Learning** process of my healing from this horrific situation. It became abundantly clear that *no* amount of money was worth my life and *no job* was worth my life. I had for six to eight months continued to travel down into a very dangerous part of Mexico all in an effort to be the best Director I could be. I truly believe in my heart that I just put the violence in a far away place whenever I was down there, even though there was not just violence but murders and assassinations every single day. As being the Head of Security was one of my roles, I would hear about these violent incidents on a daily basis. It was beyond crazy.

Whenever Yuri at Meridian Limo picked me up at the airport, I would thank my lucky stars that I had made it through another ten days of dangerous grounds, and I would sink into the plush leather seat and thank God for my life. I thanked God for giving me the strength to make it through yet another time in Mexico, relatively unscathed. And I am not a religious man, spiritual perhaps, but definitely not God-fearing. I like to think of myself as God-affirming.

Coming home to California was always the perfect time for friends, alcohol, or some "Nurse Jackie" or "True Blood", because, try as I might, I was never able to get the latest episodes down in our hacienda/hotel in Mexico. I would cook myself some American ground turkey or chicken for dinner, pour myself a glass of wine or vodka, and then relax on my beautiful blue faux-suede couch and feel so strongly that there is no place like home. It was sweet. It was delicious.

I was alive… and at that point, I was living in a beautiful one-bedroom apartment with double-height ceilings, a purple flower-covered balcony, and bizarre noises of the building's foundation settling, which sounded, at times, like poltergeists. It was my home and I loved those poltergeist moments, especially, when I had people over! It was probably my favorite apartment/home of all time. Anyway… there was nothing like being on my couch and just letting go of the violent memories of yesterday and ceasing to think about the worries of violence in a forthcoming tomorrow.

When I was home, I felt completely safe and completely secure. This priceless lesson of LOVING and APPRECIATING what you have were never more apparent than when I was lying on that couch, resting from the complete non-stop trials of Mexico… at least for a few moments… before someone else from Mexico called me. Did I mention it was a 24/7 job? It was my first 24/7-type job. That didn't bother me… it was the being kidnapped part which kinda bothered me. Thus, I left.

Being sad is perfectly okay, remember? Let me say that again for those of you who just read that as if it were just another line in a book. Being sad is perfectly okay. Being sad is a natural part of life. It is a normal and usual part of our experience of being on this Earth. I am disheartened to know that there are those who do not get sad or have not allowed themselves to be sad. How do you know what happiness feels like if you don't experience sadness! In fact, I believe that if you think really hard (or not that hard), you can probably get sad about a great deal of things. We can all do that. Stop it! Crappy things happen to us at various and many times in our lives. It is how we deal with them that builds our character and truly makes us who we are... hold that thought... to be continued in the last chapter.

I don't want to get all Marianne Williamson spiritual-politico on you now, but I do want to say a few words about the WAR that is going on inside of Mexico. Not a great deal of attention is being given to what exactly is going on there. Do you know why? It's because if a story runs about the violence, usually within the next seven to ten days, that particular journalist will somehow end up in seven or eight pieces buried near a highway, waiting to be uncovered or discovered. It happened just enough times between 2008-2010 that effectively no one would report on just how bad the violence is in a given area for fear of his or her life.

So much violence, in fact, that once in a nearby town to where we worked, there was a hold up of a robbery by a bunch of women cartel persons. They successfully managed to rob the bank, killed only a few police officers (ten to fifteen), then drove off like bats out of hell. It turns out one of the other cartels discovered their escape route and were waiting for them to drive by. There were apparently four to five cars with automatic weapons waiting for the women and, without even hesitating, brutally murdered them all, then took the money and headed off to the mountains. True story. My attorney's sister was caught in the crossfire at the bank when this occurred. Did anyone write about it? Of course not. There were essentially thirty people dead within an hour's time and no one reported a single act. Everyone in the town knew what had happened, but people just did not talk about it. That type of stuff is scary. There were curfews set directly by cartel leaders on Twitter and/or Facebook messages or articles in local newspapers. These terror messages were all set up and paid for by the local cartels. It was nuts. And clearly, so was I, for staying down there so long.

Violence is never the answer. I must say that the Mexican government has cracked down over the past five years, and have pigheadedly wanted to resolve this "situation" on its own. Mark my words, the closer the fight gets to American soil, the quicker Hillary and Obama will get involved, and then it's just a matter of time before the cartel war going on in Mexico is no longer. I am not alone in my belief system. And I doubt that neither Hillary nor Obama has any idea quite how bad the WAR has become down there. I have stayed in contact with a few people in my former region of work, and they always tell me that the "situation" has not improved. In fact, some have said, that it only gets worse with time. Someone needs to do something. The Mexican government is overrun by corruption and pompousness. They need to resolve this WAR (it's not a situation and I refuse to call it such) as soon as possible. Anyway... thank you for listening. Over 47,500 people, and counting, have lost their lives in the past five years due to this "situation". Yeah, it's not a situation. It's an all out WAR.

Shortly after my kidnapping attempt, I got a sweet-as-pie French Bulldog, or "Frenchie", named Maggie. My physician has since made her my emotional support animal and she travels with me everywhere. She works wonders and travels the world with me and my boyfriend. She is a blessing to me, my family, and this world. Maggie has been a tremendous part of my healing and learning from my experiences in Mexico. She and I are on course to complete an Animal Therapy program over the next upcoming months, so she can spread her love, adoration, and infinite happiness at hospitals.

Time was the only healer in this case and the passage thereof. It was challenging, to say the least. The best thing for me to do at the time was work on finishing my book. And that's exactly what I did, during my transition out of that position; I finished the first draft of my book. It was cathartic. It was necessary and it was such a great release.

To Be Continued...

The Day Manhattan Stood Still

September 11th cast quite the shadow on New York, D.C., and the rest of the United States. It was the first time in over sixty years that war had come to our soil. For those alive on December 7, 1941, I'm sure Pearl Harbor felt extremely similar to the events that occurred on September 11th. I know for me, it was the first time I actually felt so patriotic that I would actually fight and die for my country. And I do not believe in hatred and war, but I do believe in standing up for exactly what I believe in. Of course, at that time, I was too gay and proud to be allowed to serve openly in military. Thank God times have changed. Thank God people evolve.

Think about it, it was the largest and most deadly attack of our generation, where terrorists had infiltrated American soil. For the following four to five years until I left NYC for L.A., every time a plane would fly low over the city, I would cringe a little inside. I know I am not/was not the only person to feel that way.

My mother always had the house completely stocked. It wasn't a preparatory measure to feel safe in case of an earthquake, hurricane, or a nor'easter. Nope, it was because if she didn't have a full pantry in the house, the house wasn't complete. My mother's sister, Auntie, is the very same way. I think it must be a Jewish thing. They must have learned it from their parents, who learned it from their parents, and so on and so forth. I have noticed that both my sister and I both do the very same thing. It's just something I always did and came naturally to me. So, after 9/11, friends of mine would randomly stop by because they knew we always had tons of food to share with all of our friends. It happened several times in NYC, including on August 14th, 2003, when we completely lost power for a few days. Speaking of August 14, 2003, I will always remember that date because it is my mother's birthday… and I was very happy that I had called her earlier that morning because I wasn't able to contact her later that day.

It was about 1pm on August 14th when we lost all power in New York City and much of the Tri-State area. It was absolutely crazy. Once again, I had to walk home… this time I was again about two miles away from home. Everybody was in the streets and once again walking north. It sure reminded me of what we had all been through just two years prior. It was actually a pretty horrific site to see. This time, though, there was no ash, just tons of people. Additionally, this time, everybody was up to partying. Restaurants remained open, and it was a cash only frenzy. It was actually an amazing energy. I would venture to say that there was more energy and crazy vibes in the air than when there is electricity! In other words, the normal hustle and bustle energy of New York had subsided, and the inner hustle and bustle of New Yorkers came through loud and clear. I still maintain that there were a TON of babies conceived that very night. Anyway… people and friends came over once again; they would walk for hours to get to us because they knew we had LOTS of food. It felt awesome!

I now see that I do want to be prepared in case of any type of catastrophe. I live in Los Angeles, the capital of earthquakes. I even have an app, which tells me how many earthquakes and their magnitudes happen every day, not just in L.A., but around the world. Apparently there are earthquakes various times in one day. While living in L.A., I always feel like there are earthquakes going on… and it usually turns out to be something else. Silly me. Anyway… be it an earthquake, an asteroid, or alien invasion, I am prepared. Not just that… we also have four hens, two goats, and, for a brief period, a bunny in our backyard, so we can eat eggs, chicken, and secure goat milk for quite a while. Ok, so that is a little extreme, but now we also have an earthquake/survival kit in our garage. I think it's necessary to have an emergency plan in place because you really never do know what could happen. It is the year 2012, for Christ's sake (pun intended), and, supposedly, "the end of the world," according to the Mayan calendar. So why not be a little bit more prepared?

OK, I digressed a little, but these are all lessons, which I have learned from various disasters that have happened in and around me. For the several months following 9/11, as I mentioned, New Yorkers and their tolerance level for B.S. behavior was much less. I told you that people would stand up to crazies on the subways…

and believe me, there are a ton of them. In fact, once, I was traveling in a subway about five stops. I was sitting across from an attractive young lady… and then two seats over from her, there was a crazy individual. He kept making eyes at her and then looking at his penis area. It was horribly uncomfortable, especially when he started groping it.

There was no one around us, so, yours truly got up and pretended to be looking at the subway map and pretended like I was lost. I started asking her stupid and silly questions that anyone would know, but she got the hint quickly enough. Under my breath, I suggested she get off at the next stop and wait for the next train and I would sit down where she was. She did. I swear there was a tear in her eye. She definitely smiled from the inside and said as she left, "My hero… Thank you." True story. Oh, so the crazy guy got upset for about two minutes then left to go into the next subway car, no doubt to torture and pick on someone else. Now, I know I am not the only one to have ever done something like that… and during those first few months after 9/11, I felt that that type of action was common. Once I even heard some suit yelling at another crazy individual, telling him to get the "f" off the train and stop bothering him. It was great. When the crazy got off the train, a small crowd of us started cheering… Actually, I started clapping!

Life is way too short. We all felt it at that point. Why bother feeling uncomfortable or disrespected? All that man in the suit wanted to do was to have some peace and quiet on his way home from Wall Street. So, I applauded him. People are always ready to cheer on a hero they witness in action. Sometimes just standing is enough. Sometimes to continue to stand is the hardest choice you'll ever have to make. Trust me, it will be worth it in the end. Helping someone may never look exactly the way you planned it. Most of the time, it's even better. And sometimes, as in the case of NYC during those first few months after 9/11, doing nothing but being yourself is the only thing you can do.

Once the dust had literally settled and several months had gone by, I noticed people started to discuss their experiences of 9/11. It only lasted a few months, however, but it was an incredibly vulnerable point in New York and the nation's history. We were sharing our stories, hoping for some release, hoping for some comfort, and hoping for someone with which to share our traumatic experiences. Two of my good friends at the time were working down there. One of them had to run like hell down forty flights of stairs while the other was trapped underground with a group of about twenty people in an abandoned basement for twenty-four hours, listening to the radio and praying for someone to find them, as none of their cell phones worked.

I can't even imagine what that must have been like. She said for most of the time it was pitch black. It was an absolutely unbelievable story filled with hope and love. The greatest part about that experience for her was that she became quite clear in terms of what she wanted. Her relationship of seven years, at that point, was not really going anywhere and she realized how unhappy she had been for a while. After this incident, she made some new choices and big decisions and said goodbye to the guy. From that experience, she learned she wanted and deserved much better. I guess it's besides the fact that she now lives here in L.A. with a lesbian lover! I wish her all the best in the world.

My partner at the time worked in the World Trade Center. When we went to bed on Monday night, September 10th, he had decided to go into the office (as he was a consultant, it wasn't always necessary for him to go into the corporate headquarters on a daily basis). Apparently, that Tuesday morning, after I had left, my partner woke up late and decided not to go in that morning. That decision potentially saved his life, but what it definitely did was make sure he didn't have a horrific story of seeing individuals make the decision between jumping or burning. He would never have the trauma to live through like those who did unfortunately go into work that day.

Every story had some type of horror and **Shock** attached to it. My partner, luckily, only experienced it on the television, safely from four miles away, like most Americans. I truly believe that his intuition saved his life. Even if he would never admit, something, on some level, told him NOT to go into work that day. That's a good lesson for all of us to share... always follow your intuition. I have learned that it's the voice in your head that resonates with your heart... that's when the intuition is talking instead of your ego.

The peculiar thing about 9/11 is that by the time I had left New York at the end of 2005, no one spoke about it. We all know it happened. We all had friends who tragically perished or were traumatized by the entire terrible situation. Yet no one would speak about it. It was a rare occasion when it did come up. When it did come up, it was always a very heavy conversation, but usually a reassuring and reaffirming story. Now that it's almost eleven years later, and being in L.A., I find that it has been brought up to me about four or five times. People here talk about it more than they did in NYC. It makes perfect sense if you think about it. People out here witnessed it at a distance, whereas we, in NYC, witnessed it first hand in our city, our town, our home. Since outsiders didn't experience this tragic day first hand, they can more easily speak about what happened. For us New Yorkers, we like to be tough. Because we do not like to show defeat, vulnerability, or weakness toward anything, we're more likely to deny a bit of the impact. For Angelenos, for example, it's easier to wallow in the pain.

It is good for people to talk about it. By talking about it, we give it less power as the most traumatic event in our young American lives. It releases anxieties and fears. It is always good to talk about trauma, as it is cathartic in many ways. I'm not saying don't talk about it... I'm saying when it comes up, share. Share your experiences. Share your personal and terrible stories. It is another step in healing that we all need, and I always learn new information on how to be human when I really listen to another's interpretation of what they consider (or what we all consider, in this case) to be a traumatic event. It is what we have learned from any situation that continues to build our character. It is what we learn from past events that propel us into the newer and more advanced versions of ourselves. Lastly, it is how far we rise from these events that pave the way for greatness, happiness, and successes.

To Be Continued...

A Friend Taken Too Young

As I told you in the last chapter, four of my friends passed away within a two-year period. It was quite the grim experience. Since we are talking about **Learning** to surrender and just plain **Learning** in general, I think it apropos to speak of exactly what I learned from those four beings who left this Earth just a little too early. Death has always been a major part of my life. By the time I was eight years old, the majority of my mother's side of the family had unfortunately passed away. Even though I hadn't been to one funeral (and this is a note to all parents everywhere), it doesn't mean that I didn't feel the sadness, loss, and missing space in my heart. So there was a lot of death on the Jewish side of my family. It worried me so, at times, that I would stay up late contemplating total death. I honestly imagined myself in a black hole of nothingness for eternity. It was terribly scary and quite mind-boggling for me. This happened for years, too! I finally grew out of it when I started to memorize lines for plays, scripts, etc... and also when I decided I wanted to be vale-dictorian and get all As... which happened, by the way.

Buster. I don't want to digress too much, but I want to paint you a picture of how death has always been an intense part of my life. During those two years when friends kept dying, it was a very heavy concentration of sadness about death. I think it all started actually with the passing of my bunny, Buster. Buster Bunny and I started our incredible relationship in 1992, and I believed he lived for eleven to twelve years after that. He was amazing and such a great pet. Over the years growing up, I had had a great deal of pets and a great deal of pets' deaths. His was by far the worst for me. He had gotten me through high school, college and beyond. Buster Bunny was named after one of my favorite "Tiny Toons" characters. If you don't know who they are, look them up online, and then definitely listen to the opening song for the show. It's a great time.

Buster was a great bunny. He was black and mini-lopped, so he was about nine or ten inches spread out and he would lick my face from time to time... it was adorably cute. The reason that I bring him up is because I have lost other pets along the way too and pets' deaths can actually affect people, in some instances, as much and as challenging as people dying. It is their undying devotion and unconditional love that we miss the most. I only have unconditional love with a few persons in my life and I can tell you they will be the hardest to let go of. Don't you agree?

Buster taught me that you can play and run and play and run but at some point, you will tire and just wanna curl up inside your home (his chewed up little upside-down shoebox). Buster was always happy to come out of the cage, but was always ecstatic to be left alone too. He honestly taught me that being alone is a-okay... and that there's nothing wrong with sitting by yourself and chewing a spoonful of peanut butter.

I can remember that his front teeth were gynormous and super sharp. I was never concerned about Buster biting me until he did. I must have done something that annoyed or irritated him and he bit me. I bled everywhere... and dropped him. He was definitely as traumatized as I was by my reaction, I'm sure. Buster in that moment taught me there's nothing to fear until there's something to fear... similar to there's nothing to worry about until there's something to worry about... which is my go-to line for anyone with a cancer scare. I find that advice relatively easy to understand intelligently but extremely difficult when one must put it into practice. Thanks, Buster, for all of the wonderful "pearls", or in your case "pellets", of wisdom.

Santiago. I met Santiago through my boyfriend. He was El Salvadorian, I think. Santiago was gorgeous and young. I believe he was about twenty-four or so when we met. We were instantly connected. His attachment to everything was similar to mine; don't get too attached and have a great time. Within a few hours of sitting and chatting with him, he told me his cancer story. Bottom line, he had a giant inoperable tumor in his brain. The head of neurosurgery at Memorial Sloan-Kettering Cancer Center advised him to get his affairs in order, as he probably had no more than six to eight months to live. Well, that had been when he was twenty-one. He lived to be twenty-six before he died. He would always make a joke about that physician - how it shows how much doctors don't believe in mind over matter.

Shortly after I met him, he traveled to The Dominican Republic to live with his brother, mother, and family and to relax. He felt the hustle and bustle of NYC was just too much and it was literally killing him. Instead, he traveled to Santiago de los 30 Caballeros, about four hours north of Santo Domingo to do yoga, acupuncture, vedge, and enjoy every moment surrounded by family.

We had the pleasure of going down to visit him when he started chemo (pill form). Santiago, my ex and I traveled all around the country for ten days, even getting stuck for three days on one of the most beautiful beaches I have ever seen, right next to the Haitian border city of Pedernales. It was called "Bahía de las Águilas"... Eagles Beach... it is miles of white sand, beautiful emerald green/Caribbean sea and it is Heaven. I guess there are worse places to get trapped.

Santiago was crazy and irresistible. His happiness and go-with-the-flow attitude was infectious. He even convinced us to have a three-way with him (which was great). He led us to believe that he could drive a vehicle, which we quickly discovered was not the case as he swerved all over the crazy-ass, broken down dirt highways in the D.R. Consequently, I taught him how to drive.

After our trip to the D.R., he came to NYC twice more. One of those times, he and I slept naked together, just to be crazy and sensual. We clearly both were excited and horny the whole night... but felt completely intimate and close the next day...and nothing happened.

A few months later we got word that he passed away. It was very close to the time that Luli passed away. Ugh. It was a challenging time.

Santiago was crazy. He lived every moment as if it were his last... because every moment that he lived past the six to eight months technically was "gifted" time in his eyes. That must be an incredibly freeing way to live. And as difficult as that is for all of us to comprehend, being with him was pure delight. He was truly a great friend for those two years that I knew him. He was always *way* more concerned with the goings-on in my life than he was with his own. I loved that about him and that's one of the most important things I have absorbed from my time with him. Always ask people about their lives... engage them in their lives and their passion will uncover itself.

Santiago was also one of the most giving individuals I have ever met. He gave to everyone around him. He had so much life to give. I have also made that a part of who I am. I give to people.

Of course, one must always set boundaries and limits, but giving is a hot and unique commodity in today's world. He was fearless. He also couldn't swim but dove into some freezing water catacombs regardless. Who cares if we had to jump in and save him from drowning? The whole time he was smiling and laughing.

Santiago was the type of amazing person who, after all of the emotions and overwhelming feelings of sadness, made living with a brain tumor look easy. Don't get me wrong, he could also be the biggest diva in the world when he wanted to be… and stubborn… but for the most part, he touched me numerous times… His spiritual being had a major impact on my physical existence. Even after the sadness subsided, I always felt happy when I thought of him. Even now, I think about him fondly and with only love in my heart. He was a free bird, flying through the last good years of his life. He was awesome. Hope you're well, Santiago!

Max. Max was only seventeen. He was far too young. His mother, Barbara, was and is a very good friend of mine. She was my second mother in NYC. She was always there to lend a helping hand, a bedroom, a meal… She continues to be an incredibly amazing woman. The fact that she still gets up every morning, goes to work, and puts a smile on her face, after the tragedy that occurred in her life, is nothing short of remarkable. She had two children, Peter and Max, whom I met when they were nine and eleven, respectively. I lived with Barbara and her children for one month in college, and then at various points when I needed a place to stay. I watched Peter and Max grow up, hit puberty, and enjoy their childhood. Unfortunately, Max and his friends made one poor choice out on a boat in between the islands off of New York City; they drowned in freezing waters. It was terrible and horrific for all. He had recently instructed his father that he didn't want eulogies at his memorial service, should there be one; he wanted someone to do stand-up.

Would you believe his father actually stood up, told us this story, and then proceeded to do a stand-up comedy routine? It was so touching there wasn't a dry eye in the house, because of the laughter and because of the sadness. Max taught all of us in that room that memorial services can be fun and it's okay to laugh and smile in the face of death.

Another lesson taught to me by Max was don't take school too seriously. "It's only school. It's what you do later in life that makes you who you are." Remember, this was a twelve-year old kid telling me that. He advised me not to pressure my kids too much to fall in my valedictorian footsteps. I promised him I would not. Go Max! Love you!!!

Vinnie. Where do I even begin with Vinnie? Let me just say that he was Judy Garland's personal stylist back in the day. Not only that - he was a trendsetter at Studio 54. He was the most famous openly gay stylist of the eighties. Thus, he always had to look his best and walk in to Studio 54 fearlessly (and with an entourage). Everyone was in awe, well, that's according to his stories!

Vinnie taught me many, many things. Vinnie was a true gentleman, always ready to listen, always ready to lend a hand, always ready to tell a story. Vinnie was in so many words, fabulous. He taught me how to be fabulous, how to live fabulously.

In his country home, he would change the entire look of several rooms as the seasons changed. Vinnie always told me to be who I am at every minute because people will always respond to authentic relationships and my cute smile. Oh, yeah, and he also taught me that it's okay to live in haunted houses, as long as you know what you are doing. His house was beyond haunted and I was extremely scared to stay there because of all of the creepy feelings I got in every room.

The most amazing gift Vinnie gave to me was through his death experience. He taught me that families come in all shapes and all sizes. It just requires a ton of hard work and communication. Family had always been of the utmost importance to him. He married a woman young, had two beautiful children, and then, mid-way through their marriage, came out to his family as gay. It was a challenging time for the first few years, but eventually the family healed and grew even tighter. Amidst all of his lovers, the family remained close as he was an openly gay father, doing his best to love and honor them.

On his deathbed, his family surrounded him 24/7. There was always someone in the bedroom with him for those last final days. I was honored enough to be witness to his beautiful family and their amazing connection. The moment he died, everybody in that family felt it. At the very moment he died in a beautiful house in Long Island at 5:45pm, his country house in upstate New York telephoned our country house. We didn't discover this until several days afterward, but it was, in my opinion, his way of saying goodbye to J (one of his best friends) and myself. I mean, I told you the house was haunted, right?

Luli. Luli was the definition of a lady. She was unique in every way. Born Ecuadorean, she was a princess in every right. Her death had more impact on me than all of the others. She was graceful in almost everything she did. I think tennis, perhaps, was the only activity she engaged in where grace escaped her. She was giving. She was honest. Luli was sincere and full of love for the world, her family, and everyone around me. Luli taught me to be graceful. She actually was one of the first ladies to show me why the word GRACE is one of my absolute favorite words in the English language. I believe it was Luli who showed me how to be soft and be vulnerable in front of other people. Very few things were a BIG deal to her and I LOVED that about her... so I decided to embody that easy-goingness from her!

Up until that point, my "college life" consisted of one dramatic incident after the next without pause. Ecuador was an unbelievable break from all that drama. Even when I got punched in that underground gay bar for no apparent reason, it still was not an overly dramatic experience. Somehow being around Luli, my drama became less and less dramatic.

Luli walked the walk and talked the talk. Again, she was not a saint and she definitely had her faults, like that American boyfriend of hers. He was a douchebag! (I have to digress for just a second here. Douchebag was Miley Rae a/k/a Miley Cyrus' favorite word circa 2009. Oh, did I mention that I had the occasion to hang out with her a couple times? When I broke up with Paolo, she even called me a douchebag! She was an interesting individual. At one point, she would be dancing around like a 16-year-old, and the next moment, she would be holding an extremely deep conversation about life.) Anyway... I'm sure Luli's ex (the one we were never fond of) is much better and very different by now, but Luli had something awful for him in his douchebag heyday. We are all blinded by love... so I swore

I would never be *that* blinded to love, especially if NONE of my friends like the partner.

Through her love of the family and her sister, she exemplified what a sister could be (except when the douchebag was around). Did I make my point about him? Anyway, Luli was elegance. She was beauty and beautiful and her energy was infectious. She would always laugh at my jokes and politely correct my Spanish when it was incorrect. I love her and miss her. I think about her a lot, to be honest. I believe she is always with me.

It was a few days after I had grossly broken down in my bathroom when I had my first experience talking to a dead loved on. I had never really done it before and though it would terrify probably anyone, I felt extremely at peace during and after the encounter. See, I had missed one train and decided to take the long way to work, to walk a little further than normal, as it was a beautiful day outside. I very much enjoyed the fresh air in late April, early May. I was walking and smiling and enjoying my own business when I felt Luli's presence all around me. I proceeded to talk to her as if she were there with me. I figured I could either ignore it or I could surrender to the present moment and perhaps make contact or peace. I don't specifically remember the dialogue and it was all in my mind. I do remember she wanted me to take care of her family, especially her sister, who is still one of my best friends. She wanted me to be happy and know that it doesn't matter how she died (as there was a little bit of confusion surrounding the exact cause) but that she was in a much better place and she wanted me to help her family to see that. Her energy left as quickly as I had first felt it. I felt such peace and love after that for days and days. Thank you, Luli for giving me that gift. I will hopefully return the favor some day. Luli meant a great deal to me and her death meant a great deal to me too. Stay tuned as next chapter I conclude Luli's passing with angels and my visit to Ecuador…

To Be Continued…

5 THINGS TO REMEMBER WHEN IN LEARNING

1.   It Could ALWAYS Be Worse!

Hear me now. Listen to what I'm saying to you. It could be worse. I know this might be hard to hear right now, but really, it could ALWAYS be worse. Really? Really.

2.   Time is Always on Your Side!

Take time. Time is always on your team, routing for you. Take the time you need for yourself. Even if you are the President of the United States, almost anything can wait one more hour, one more day, or even 48 hours.

3.   Share your Story.

It is your story and your life. Tell it often. Relish in the fact that no one can ever take that experience or event away from you. It is yours and you have grown past it. I believe every time we share our story, we heal a little bit more and release it into the Universe (or give it a little bit more to God, if that tickles your fancy).

4.   Live on "Gifted" time.

We can all take away an incredible lesson from Santiago and live as if we are on "gifted" time. It sounds beautiful, doesn't it? It also sounds nearly impossible! Be a little happier. Be a little bit more patient. Love life. Love everyone. Sounds like a great place to me.

5. Choose to Be Happy.

Be unique. Be different. You can choose at each moment to be happy. I know, I know. Remember earlier in this chapter, I alluded to the fact that one could choose his or her day? Same idea... at any moment, you can choose to have a different emotion. I am not saying don't feel sad or depressed... nay, I encourage you to feel every feeling. At the same time know that you do have control over your feelings and how long you decide to experience each emotion/feeling.

LEARNING: In Conclusion

"Ohhh... Wow!" - In this stage, we are **Learning** to surrender: to "be". We are **Learning** to live with whatever's going on. **Learning** is how we know we are on the strong path to healing. **Learning** is how we know that the worst is over and it's now time to get up, move on, and live life to the fullest.

Time is a gift. Time heals. Sometimes even time takes time, and patience takes patience. Time is the one universal concept always on our side.

Taking the time to reflect on our **Learning** is of *crucial* importance if we want to heal from anything. Realizing the truth of any situation is vital to the discovery and uncovering, which allows the opportunity and space for healing and growth. Really, it's all about the lessons you learn. These lessons usually prevent us from making the same choices again. It usually prevents us from even being close to that same or similar circumstance again.

Obviously, some incidents are out of our control. And for those instances, you still have the choice of how to grieve, how to be sad, how to feel emotion, and how to move on. Or you can laugh. I believe we all need to laugh more. Laugh until you cry. Laugh until it hurts. Laugh like you are coming out of a "Mexicoma" - thanks, *Sex and The City* movie!

Learning is essential to the process. It is necessary to acknowledge those particular lessons learned. It is necessary to feel the emotions, go through the motions, and then come to this place of knowing. This place is where the emotions subside and the true feelings and **Learning** reveal themselves. It can be a very taxing process, if you let it, or it can be a truly great experience filled with a tremendous amount of feedback. Without the acknowledgement and validation of your situation at hand, you cannot proceed to the next level or the next step... which is to **Embrace** all that has happened to you.

Learning to surrender to the situation is one of the most challenging things one will ever do. **Learning** to surrender happens when one is present enough to see the situation from a non-biased perspective and to see one's role and responsibility therein. The moment you see the responsibility is the very moment you start the **Learning** process and therefore pave the way for the final step for Smiling From The Inside.

The moment you see the craziness for the craziness that it is, is the very moment you start the healing process. In my experience, this is where most people get stuck. They get stuck in their own narrative or perception. They get stuck because they do NOT take responsibility for their actions or behaviors. So many people get stuck in this phase and never move on to experience the lightness, serenity, and power on the other side. Believe me, it is quite a release once the B.S. fades, the blame subsides, and the anger dissipates. It allows more space and more opportunity for amazing things to happen. **Learning** to surrender allows the mind to clear, the body to heal, and the soul to cleanse.

As every yogi realizes with arm balances, it takes many attempts, many, many falls, and laughing is definitely required. You just cannot take it all too seriously. The key to arm balances is full body memory. In other words, amidst all the mistakes, the falls, the almost theres, finally, one day it just clicks and the body remembers how to reconstruct the position naturally. It remembers what to do and what not to do. This should sound a little bit familiar and remind you of the **Learning** stage in the S.M.I.L.E. Method for healing.

Learning from your mistakes is a wonderful way to retain valuable information. It can be what differentiates you from the rest of the individuals around you. The process of **Learning** is the place where warm-ups (**Shock**), practice and conditioning (**Mock-cceptance**), and the emotional superhighway (**In Overwhelmdom**) converge to teach you wise lessons, thereby easing your ability to deal with all of life's little obstacles. Thus, it's the second-to-last step we all must surmount to live a more comfortable and more insightful Smile From The Inside life.

EMBRACE

STAGE FIVE: EMBRACE.

Embrace

verb

1. hold (someone) closely in one's arms, especially as a sign of affection: *[with object] Aunt Sophie embraced her warmly. [no object] The two embraced, holding each other tightly.*

2. accept (a belief, theory, or change) willingly and enthusiastically: *Besides traditional methods, artists are embracing new technology.*

3. include or contain (something) as a constituent part: *His career embraces a number of activities - composing, playing, and acting.*

noun

1. an act of holding someone closely in one's arms: *They were locked in an embrace.*

2. used to refer to something which is regarded as surrounding, holding, or restricting someone: *Totalitarianism has meant that no interest falls outside the embrace of the state.*

3. *[in singular]* an act of accepting something willingly or enthusiastically: *Their eager embrace of foreign influences*[11].

Expressed Feeling = "Yeehaw!"

Please review the definition of the word **Embrace** above. To **Embrace** is to accept without judgment, to accept without fear (or maybe just a little fear), and to accept with love and grace. Acceptance is a beautiful and scary place. We are always striving for acceptance in order to **Embrace** whatever has happened to us in the past. Embracing goes much further than just accepting. It is the celebration of you, who you are now, where you've come from, and where you are going. Thus the phrase, **"Yeehaw!"**

Acceptance just isn't enough anymore.

Acceptance happens when reality comes into clear focus. Reality is very scary for most people. Actually, it's a little bit scary for all of us. I haven't had the fortune or misfortune to participate heavily with drugs, so I have gotten used to reality. Of course, I am O.C.D. about some things, so sometimes I get anxious because of reality. In order for me to deal with that

---

11   "Embrace," OxfordDictionary.com, 2012.

anxiety, I do silly things like make sure I am in the right lane about 3-4 blocks prior to making a right turn. You know? We all have our issues, right?

Acceptance is going beyond coming to terms with what is. It is the final entryway just before the very last step of the S.M.I.L.E. healing process. Acceptance does not necessarily equal happiness. To move toward a place of happiness or contentment, one must **Embrace** what has happened completely and move forward with life. Look forward to the next phase of your life! Believe that love is out there somewhere for you! If you are still looking for your next ex, then perhaps turn back to the previous chapter! If you are looking for the next best friend, companion, and lover but are feeling a little fearful of it all, now you are getting it! We are all in this together. It is a struggle for all of us.

If you look at the definition of **Embrace** again, you will notice the word "enthusiasm." Enthusiasm is something that I have infinitely flowing through my body. If you know me, you can attest to that fact. I believe in happiness! I believe in inner peace! Most of all, what works for me is my belief in contentment. I speak of contentment because these electrifying and appreciative moments are a great sign of the fifth phase, **Embrace**. Contentment, by my definition, is happiness and inner peace wrapped into one. I know that most of us seek happiness. Sometimes, I feel like happiness can come with a load of expectations, whereas if you think about contentment, contentment is a culmination of sweeping moments where there are bursts of happiness, shots of glee, and splurges of love.

Contentment for me is walking down the street, on a beautiful sunny day, listening to the "Don't Stop Believing" remix by the *Glee* cast (love you guys!), and realizing that I am actually a very lucky guy. On my way to acupuncture, I continue bobbing my head and thinking I have a good job, a partner who is crazy, but who challenges me every day; I have a lovely roof over my head; I have some very good friends; and I have an amazing backyard filled with goats, pigs, chickens, bunnies, and Maggie, my Frenchie. Those pockets of contentment occur without warning and without thinking. I guarantee you it happens. It doesn't mean you won't be sad from time to time, but contentment is what I strive for each and every day. I don't necessarily get there, but I KNOW it's there if I want it. Those moments of contentment occur more and more often for those who practice the art of Smiling From The Inside.

Some people are masters of self-sabotage, as we all are from time to time, but some more than others. Those who self-sabotage take specific actions, which cause negative attention, or participate in the dramatic and provocative parts of life. These people lack enthusiasm, contentment, and acceptance. But those people can change, too!

Some people can never be "happy" for very long, as it is uncomfortable. I know so many people that are awkward in their own skin. Unfortunately, you will never be content if you feel discomfort within. That's just how the stuff works. I hope those people have picked up a copy of this book. Perhaps it can help.

Everything in life is a choice. We can change the course of our lives with every new choice that comes our way. We can choose to **Embrace** everything that is given to us in our lives or we can choose to fight it. I believe that the Universe/God does not give us more than we can handle. Sometimes, I know, I have my doubts, but in the end, we can overcome anything. You can choose to go to school, or you can play hooky. (A quick aside, I never played hooky in high school. No. Instead, my mother and I called them "mental health days." Come on, I was a straight-laced, straight-A, valedictorian of a student. I intend to do the very same with my own kids.) Essentially, you can choose to learn from each and every situation, or you can choose not to learn. It's your decision.

You have gone through the worst, and now it is time to focus on you and your future. You can always do small things to make yourself a little happier each day! The clouds are lifting and there is blue sky. About three years ago, I remember two weeks when it rained almost every day here in L.A. That is extremely rare, considering we get about a dozen days of rain per year. What amazed me most about Los Angeles was that even throughout the biggest storm we'd had in years, at every possible chance given, the sun would break through, if only for about twenty minutes. It was glorious… and my favorite part of the entire experience of the storm. I tend to think of us humans in that sense. We are sometimes so bogged down by the pain, hurt, and sadness, that it's hard to let the light shine through. Remember, even in those times of darkness, I believe, we, as humans, are always meant to shine. I think it is in our nature to shine and smile. So, be bold, shine and smile. **Embrace** your past, your present, and your future. I know. I know. Easier said than…

As **Shock** acts as the warm-up, **Mock-cceptance** helps the mental and physical you through conditioning, **In Overwhelmdom** pushes you to your emotional limits, and **Learning** allows you the opportunity to physiologically and psychologically process,

Embrace facilitates the enthusiastic acceptance, appreciation, and acknowledgement of the unexpected event that you have just experienced. Master all of the above and you will be certain to live a Smile From The Inside life.

At the end of every yoga class, you may have seen people lying on the floor. It's actually a pose called Savasana (dead corpse pose). The object is to clear your mind, calm your body, and relax into the experience of being you.

In the final installment of my very personal stories, you will see the power behind **Embrace** as the last step in the S.M.I.L.E. Method for healing. When you can **Embrace** everything you have learned along the way, your possibilities in life will be unlimited. Much like coming out of Savasana, you will feel alive and energized, two more ideas integral to the Smile From The Inside lifestyle.

Um… You Lost Me at Cancer

Linda Mechanic, the master potter, was an inspiration to me. That day when I finally went to pick up our poor version of bowls, Linda briefly told me of her struggles with cancer: two rounds of breast cancer, and one round of ovarian cancer. She definitely had it rough. The idea had been scurrying in my head for years to write a book featuring fellow cancer survivors and hearing their amazing and harrowing tales. Immediately, I set up a date with her to hear her stories and start my book. A few weeks later, we met up, and I recorded the entire conversation. I have done nothing yet with my recorded sessions, but I will.

At first, she told me about her two rounds with breast cancer…
scary! Then, she spoke of her ovarian cancer. The breast cancer
was a piece of cake compared to the ovarian cancer. Let's be honest, the survival rate for ovarian cancer is quite poor compared
to other cancers. It was extremely touching, especially as she
relayed a story about when she was in the hospital for several
weeks in 2009. She wanted me to share with the world just how
important snail mail had become to her and can be for anyone.
Apparently, a couple of her friends got together and decided to
each send her a card. That card would contain a real life photo
of them holding a candle in her honor. News spread like wildfire
and within fourteen days, Linda had received over one hundred
cards with incredible candle photos. She and her partner created
a book of the photos. Linda made it known to me with fervor
and passion that those (what seemed to be) little gestures from
people can propel someone's mind from reactive to proactive.
She firmly believed that those candles saved her life, and so do I.
We had a great time together and became quite close after that
touching story.

Over the next year or so, Linda and I kept in touch, having
lunch every few months… and she seemed to be doing pretty
well for having ovarian cancer. She and I would laugh… I called
myself a "Cancer Lite" case compared to her history of cancer!
For our incredible lunches, Linda would always want to focus
on me first, and then the conversation would naturally turn
back to her and I would hear the latest cancer update. She definitely had her ups and downs over the next two years. She was
always willing to give me sisterly advice and would *always* tell
me the God's honest truth every time about any issue I might
have been facing.

In 2010, when Oprah's network, OWN, was searching for persons to host a show, Linda was the one who convinced me that I needed to audition. And, boy, did she help me out! Not only was Linda an amazing cancer survivor guest on my audition tape, but also she was integral throughout the entire editing process. I was just about finished when she suggested a complete change to the four-minute video. As pissed as I was to return and do over almost everything, the video came out fabulous. It was overall an amazing experience. She loved the audition video so much, she placed it on her pottery website. Linda was a gem of a human, giving to the very last drop. Clearly, I didn't win, but I got a decent amount of votes... and hopefully, someday soon, I will be discovered as an amazing personality to have my own show. Thank you, Linda.

The last time I saw Linda was with my current partner, Adam. It was three weeks before Adam, a physician of internal medicine, was due to undergo a major surgery. He was secretly terrified about the upcoming surgery and she could feel it. We spent the majority of the time speaking of the repercussions... and of the pros and cons of having a colostomy bag. It was quite an intense conversation. The whole time, though, I knew she was hiding something. Toward the end of our lunch, she admitted that her ovarian cancer had come back twice as hard.

Linda gave one look to Adam, someone who had treated patients in similar circumstances many times, and he knew what that meant, but I didn't. I was in a bit of disbelief. It doesn't look good was all she said about it. This strong and courageous woman allowed herself one tear. The table fell silent... all except for Maggie, who was by Adam's feet throughout the entire conversation, and who, moved by the sadness in the air, went over to Linda and jumped up on her, as if to say never give up, lady! It was a great moment and we all laughed. There's nothing like laugh therapy or animal therapy, for that matter.

Saying goodbye to Linda was always a bit hard because I enjoyed her energy so much. That time, it seemed unbearable to me. Looking back, I think I knew that that could be the last time I might ever see her. That was July of 2011.

I reached out to her in late September, and she replied that she was laying low because of the cancer. A few weeks later, I texted her in mid-October to ask when our next lunch would be and to tell her how much I adored and loved her. She responded that night, saying only "Seth…" to which I responded "Hi!!!!" Her second to last text to me was "We will talk later. Been in hospital since Sunday. Getting ready to go home today. Tired." I knew what that meant. It doesn't take a genius to figure out that she was going home to die. I found out from her partner that she actually remained in the hospital for one more week… and so I wanted to send her flowers. I texted for her address. Her very last text to me included just her address on October 22, 2011.

I hadn't received word back regarding the flowers until a few days later when her girlfriend facebooked me that the flowers had put a huge smile on her face. I fully expected her to recover, at least enough for me to be able to see her again in November.

Unfortunately, in November, I went to India for two weeks to accompany Adam on a medical mission trip all over the country, and it was more than halfway through my trip when I learned of

Linda's passing... and of how I had completely missed her funeral. God... was I ever upset. I was angry, sad, and felt cheated. I wanted to spend so much more time with her... and I told her I would be there to help her die in one of our many encounters. She probably didn't think I was serious, but I was.

It was quite the loss. I don't know whether it was the ten days in a row of Indian food or the news of her death that made me sick for the last three days of my trip. I think it was a little bit of both. I wasn't completely surprised, but I had really wanted to be there for the funeral. I wrote a loving letter to her partner, and in her response, she advised me that in the early spring, they would hold a memorial service and I could say my goodbyes then. Time flew by. Before I knew it, the day of the memorial service had arrived.

As some of you know, from time to time, I feel energies around me. This has pretty much been throughout my whole life, but only until recently have I been able to **Embrace** it. Linda was definitely there in spirit and in rare form. I didn't see her, but I felt her... as did many people in the room. She stayed by me for most of my time there. I was imagining that she was making her usual witty remarks to make me laugh... which didn't appear all that appropriate considering that there were people in tears all around me. She was amazed by all of the people that had come to say goodbye... and was beyond herself laughing that she had created that much love and support in her lifetime. I told her, I expected more people! It was honestly as if we were having a conversation... or perhaps it was all in my head. Whatever you choose to believe, she was there on some level or another.

Now, I had NO intention of saying anything or sharing anything about our relationship, as it was definitely a whirlwind… but she, or the spirit of Linda, pushed me to speak. I usually like to be extra prepared in situations like that… but something kept telling me if I spoke from the heart, it would be ten times more impactful. Most people had notes, papers, etc… I just went up there with nothing. For what felt like 20 minutes (in actuality it was more like 5 minutes), I spoke and shared the stories that I thought or felt Linda wanted me to share. Everyone laughed. Everyone cried.

Toward the very end of my "speech," I was overcome with emotion and tears. I gracefully finished my last thought and proceeded to walk off the "stage"… and the room went into an uproar. Apparently, my speech was well received. Her partner came up to me and gave me the biggest hug EVER… as well as her sister and a whole bunch of people I didn't even know. Was Linda somehow speaking through me? No… but she definitely gave me suggestions and insights. I received so many accolades for my little speech, I felt extremely at peace… and I knew that both Linda and her partner were definitely grateful to hear words of love from this little gay boy who had fallen in love with a beautiful and inspirational lesbian potter.

Did I have closure? Yes. Did I feel better? Oh, yes. That day, I spoke about what I had learned from Linda and who she had been to me. And I knew she had been equally as sacred to anyone and everyone in that room. At that moment, even through all of the emotions, sadness, and laughter, I was able to really **Embrace** not only my own experience with Cancer, but what was going on… and just go with it.

I miss Linda terribly. And even while writing this, I have shed many tears… which means… that I am human. When I get sad, I cry. And this human always does the best that he can.

It is now almost six years after my cancer scare. I have been cancer free ever since. (Knock on wood!) I have completely accepted my cancer and I have learned to **Embrace** it as part of my specialness in this lifetime. It has become part of my history and part of my experience as a spiritual existence in this human body. I, of course, have my moments when the feelings and emotions pop up again, but I gladly allow them to surface, and I treat them kindly, especially when I watch movies that have some type of protagonist with cancer, and sometimes it might even take me a few moments to collect my thoughts and feelings, but always do. I take care of myself. I take care of my emotions and feelings, because they do go deep. I accept them as part of me. I **Embrace** the feelings as my own and as special ones at that. It makes me feel alive and whole when the feelings surface once in a while.

To **Embrace** one's past does not mean to disregard it, and it certainly doesn't mean to forget it. I remember everything about my experience and I am thankful that it happened. I am appreciative to have been given the opportunity to know *that* anguish and *that* sorrow, so the happiness and contentment can shine that much brighter. **Embracing** my past clears the space to allow new adventures and new experiences to further shape who and what I am. Every experience helps to shape the essence of who and what we are. Cancer schmancer. I have lived another day to tell my story and some others as well!

I Thought We Were Monogamous!

I gotta be honest; up until these last few weeks, I have had a very hard time accepting or **Embracing** the situation that occurred with Paolo. I am not even convinced that I might ever be 100% there to completely and fully **Embrace** what happened in our relationship. And that's okay too! And now back to the story, Life is always filled with crazy twists and turns. Yes, I cheated on him... several times in one week, in fact. This was my way of breaking free. I'm not proud at all.

I thought that if I got him to break up with me, I could actually start to heal from everything that we had been through. I thought that if he grew upset and ended things in a vicious manner (which I had secretly anticipated from the beginning), it would make it that much easier to walk away. That being said, I clearly did not mean for our break-up to hurt him quite as much as it did. But, come on, folks, let's be honest, he was cheating on me left and right, and he nearly gave me the Human Immunodeficiency Virus. Moreover, Paolo's hailing from another culture reminded me of the prevalent blatant hypocritical and machismo behavior that exists in other countries, where it is socially acceptable for a man to cheat on his wife anytime he wants, but it's not okay for the wife to step out on the husband. A different culture. A very different perspective on love.

At the time of confessing my indecent behaviors to him, I still believed Paolo when he said that he had NOT cheated on me once. I later discovered this to be patently false. How did I find out? A couple months after Paolo and I broke up, I hooked up with someone who openly admitted that Paolo and he had hooked up back when we were together. I really didn't believe him at first, but then he explained more of the situation and what had happened. I was confused. I got a little angry... and frankly it ruined my night. I felt a little sick. And then I realized what a dork Paolo had been, what a silly-head I had been, and, boy, was I glad to be out of that relationship.

Would you believe, he contends to this day that he NEVER cheated on me. I know I have related this before, but I just want to reiterate that point to underscore how naïve - and arguably sad, or hurt, one must be to actually *continue lying* when the truth has been out there for quite some time.

I keep telling myself it's not my issue anymore, it's his...which is the truth. It still bothers me a tiny bit, I'm not going to lie. Things like that are very hard to overcome and even harder to let go. First, I had to come to terms with the fact that I had moved beyond the relationship. I learned a great deal from it, and now, two years later, I am still moving on to bigger and better pastures. Secondly, I had to tell myself many *many* times that his problems were not my problems. Lastly, I learned to appreciate the fact that he did NOT give me HIV and I was lucky to be alive and would live each day to the fullest. Sometimes life cannot be wrapped up into a pretty little bow. Sometimes we have to continuously and perpetually work through some particular issues such as this one. It stinks, but every day gets a little bit easier.

If I sound a bit bitter, perhaps I am. I was very angry at the situation then yes. I also learned a great deal from the situation, yes. Did I cheat because I was angry? Not exactly, I cheated cause I had nothing to lose and I wanted to feel intimate with someone – no strings attached. I wanted to be kissed by someone and I wanted to feel special again. That is why I cheated. That was and had always been a recurring theme in my behavior when I felt trapped and there was no way out. Our couple's therapy sessions clearly could not save us. I like to think that when I'm in an incredibly special relationship, I would NEVER feel the need to cheat.

During my last few relationships, I found myself always encouraging and challenging the other person to be the best that they could be... all the while, getting less independent - and even shafted - on my side. Coming from a place of full responsibility, I allow myself to get deep into these co-dependent relationships, where I spend so much time trying to fix the other person, I forget who I am and I give them my power. I have recently uncovered that in intimate relationships, my pattern has been to recreate my parents' healthy forty-two year interdependent relationship in an unhealthy manner. I want to heal my partners from their very dynamic pasts and in return (or the pay off is), they need me. Not anymore! Naturally, once I break up with someone, within two to four months, I am my own extremely strong self again, reminding myself once again of how amazing I am and how much I have to give.

It is a pattern that is particularly hard to break, but I am now finally aware. That said, I know now that I want someone who is relatively whole. I don't mind if they have had an extreme and colorful past, I care how they have dealt with it and how it has shaped them into this tremendous person that stands before me. That has been my journey and **Learning** through this situation. That has been my process to **Embrace**. As explained previously, sometimes I do not choose the healthiest individuals, because something inside tells me I can help them to grow into healed souls. Sometimes, I refer to it as my "savior complex". I feel like I can heal the world. I do believe that, but I have no knack for healing the person with whom I choose to share my life and experiences and that's a drag. It's just not my purpose or my place anymore.

I believe the moment I started to accept what had happened to me and Paolo was the day I woke up and finally told him that he just wasn't enough for me and that I deserved much better in my life. Ouch. I know. Harsh. When the promise of staying with him started to completely compromise my lifelong happiness, inner light, and joy, I felt I could no longer honor my previous promise to him, if I was going to be true to myself. I chose to escape from our sinking ship. He was not capable of loving me even remarkably close to the way I loved him. Paolo had a great deal of healing to do from his troubled and multi-colored past... wounds that went deep and had a powerful hold over him. When I realized I couldn't take it anymore, I slept on it for three days prior to telling him the truth about the end of our relationship. Wanting to be clear, it was probably a bit harsh, but the truth *can* hurt.

In the end, his best just wasn't good enough for me. Let me say that one more time so everyone, even the back row, can hear me. In the end, his best just wasn't good enough for me. I don't believe there is just one person for each of us and I don't believe in staying with anyone who isn't good enough for you, either. I believe in challenging times, yes. I believe in patience, working through some of your issues, and exploring temporary options to resolve permanently ingrown behavioral patterns. But please keep asking yourself, at what cost? If it compromises who you are, you better take a good look at yourself. You can always get out. You can always choose differently. It will hurt, for sure. As I always say, **Pain is Inevitable, but Suffering is Optional**. Be true to yourself. Always be the best of yourself you can be. Always treat yourself better than anyone and everyone else. Love yourself. **Embrace** yourself. It will be worth it in the end. Trust me.

If you keep running back toward the person you need to run away from, you'll never create the space for better things to arrive.

I moved out the next day, and have never looked back. We still text from time to time, because we made a choice to purchase a vehicle together, after only being together for a year. We are almost done with that situation. I truly believe once that last financial transaction between us is complete, I will be able to distance myself 100% from him. Perhaps then, will I be able to look back, fully accept, then **Embrace** our relationship.

Hindsight is really a great tool to learn what to do the next time around. Back to two years ago, there comes an inherent freedom in being single. It means freedom to do nothing – freedom to do everything. You have the freedom to eat whenever you want to and the freedom to bed whomever you want to. There was no pressure from anyone to do anything. I was not scared of what the night would bring or scared of the mood someone might bring home. It was just me. I could rest if I wanted, cry if I wanted, or just laugh silly. OMG… it was glorious.

Of course, we all want partnership. However, the elation and freedom that comes from breaking up with some bad ju-ju is bittersweet. It's bittersweet because on the one hand, you are definitely free. On the other hand, you have just broken up with someone and your emotions are all over the place. After the intense emotions subside, and the surrender takes place, there is a great sense of power and freedom. That's where the acceptance and the embracing comes in. It's okay to be torn. It's okay to take your time in healing. Clearly, it's taken me a long time to get to where I am now, and I am still uncovering layers with regard to Paolo.

When you can look at a past event with little emotion and see it at every angle without judgment and with full responsibility, then the Smile From The Inside work is coming to an end. Writing this book has been extremely cathartic for me. I haven't quite surrendered to everything with regard to this particular past event, but I'm working on it. Writing this has given me the strength, courage, and feelings I needed to release, preparing me for the final **Embrace** of this experience. It still brings up a great deal of emotions within me... and perhaps thinking about it always will. This situation, you have to admit, is a doozy. There are a lot of unanswered questions, and it was dirty. Sometimes life will be like that... where there are no answers, and it will be dirty. We just do the best we can.

Life is not pretty sometimes, but it's how well we pick up the paintbrush and start brushing again that matters. Sometimes you may feel like you can't win and other times you may feel like you can't lose. Who cares about winning or losing? Play the game hard. Play the game of life to the best of your ability. Crappy things will happen and wonderful things will happen. Feel the intense and overwhelming emotions. Do not shy away from emotion. Surrender. Learn what you can learn, and then accept and

Embrace the situation. Who cares if it brings up some emotions when you speak or write about it? Again, it is only residue. It's always about letting more residues go. It's always about telling your story, releasing your final emotions, just getting it out... getting it all out.

I think it makes it a bit harder to accept all of this when your ex continues to make your life challenging and continues to play old roles, which is what Paolo has done with regard to our vehicle. Some people just never learn... and sometimes it's easier to be nice to someone just long enough to get what you need prior to kicking them out of your life forever. I don't necessarily agree with kicking people out of your life forever, but in certain circumstances, I definitely think it's worth it to distance yourself from them for a couple of months, a couple of years, or as long as you wish. I always encourage forgiveness for everyone, most of all for ourselves. Forgiving, as difficult as you may consider it, is actually one of the major keys to inward happiness, passion, freedom, and contentment. Forgiveness can set you free. It's all freeing. And freedom is a prerequisite to the Smile From The Inside model. It can give you wings and can carry you anywhere you want to go. Be clear in your forgiveness and be clear in your heart.

I must admit that even as I write this, I am breathing heavily and releasing more residue with each exhale. Slowly and surely the process of healing will work for me. While I may have not completely **Embraced** what happened with Paolo and his sero-conversion, I can tell you I have accepted what happened between us. I can also tell you that every time I talk about it, share it, and postulate about it, it gets better for me and little bit easier to let more of it go. Life isn't always as black and white! It's a constant work in progress. I am working on it. I am doing the work and I fully intend, one day, to **Embrace** it *all*. And you can too!

Un Secuestro en México – A Kidnapping in Mexico

How do you know when you've **Embraced** an issue? The fact that I will never step foot in Mexico again… does that mean that I've **Embraced** what happened to me? No. It means that I value my life. That's completely my choice and my prerogative. It's a little dramatic… and I might go back at some point in my life, because it is a beautiful country filled with mountains, rivers, lakes, warm people, etc. This might be the first time I have admitted out loud that I would even consider returning to Mexico. To be honest, I met some of the greatest friends a guy could ever ask for… So, have I **Embraced** it? Yes, I believe I have. What does that even mean? It means that I have looked at the situation from every angle and still view it the same way. It means that I can talk about it openly and freely. It means that I can laugh about it, cry about it, or smile about it.

I have talked about my almost kidnapping in many situations. It comes up in every job interview, when the interviewer asks me the reason why I left my favorite job in my whole career. Some have suggested I say there was a dangerous incident and that's why I decided to leave, but depending on the audience, everyone loves drama and everyone loves details… especially hearing interesting stories that open and expand their minds and beliefs. In job interviews, I briefly share my story, unless they want details, details,

details. I can discuss what happened to me without much attachment. My emotions don't usually rise up. I might get goose bumps once in a while, but I don't get flustered anymore. I have accepted this story as my own and, to be honest, it definitely is an interesting story and makes me a more interesting human.

I firmly believe that everything happens for a purpose. I had about seven job interviews last week, all of which I felt went very well and here I am writing this, with perhaps no offers. I have a few choices. 1) I can either be completely depressed about it, which is the easiest thing to do. I can wallow in my disappointment for the next few hours, days, or weeks. 2) I can choose to be disappointed, but keep going strong. I can keep submitting resumes and applying to all of the suitable jobs. Or, 3) I can be a little sad, accept it, realize that something great will come along, and be happy for everything else that's great in my life. Also, I can choose to see this as a sign. A sign that the right thing just hasn't presented itself yet and trust the universe/God. I can trust that God knows what He is doing... and the greatest job for me will arrive when it is the right time.

I really am excited to find my next job, and cross that search off my list, so I can focus on what makes me happy, what gives me such strength, and what inspires me. I am a little less sad now. I know that if it had been meant to happen, it would have happened. I'm actually getting excited about my next gig. I know that good things are going to happen to me. It just might take a few more hours or days to see that clearly. The most challenging thing to do right now is to enjoy this process! I enjoy telling people I was almost kidnapped. I enjoy telling people that my ex sero-converted and that I had cancer. Why? I enjoy telling people because it confirms that I am a strong individual and an inspiring survivor. It reaffirms to me and to everyone else that I have an incredible amount of inner-strength and gumption. I can survive anything. Absolutely anything that's put in my way!

I adore that about myself, that in spite of all the "stuff" that has happened or that might happen, I KNOW I am going to be better than ever. I truly believe that it could always be worse. I want to impress upon everyone reading this that your best is yet to come. I'm going to repeat that statement because it is so important. Your best is always yet to come. Remember that. Remember that for the rest of your lives. When sad things happen, remind yourself, that this is temporary and it will pass. With regard to the almost kidnapped, it has become a part of me. It has become just a story and a tale. It's a tale that gives me strength, a tale that teaches a lesson, and the very dramatic end to the amazing journey that was my position in Mexico. All that being said, I can tell you that very rarely does a day pass when I don't think about the almost kidnapping. Re-living it makes me feel alive and it makes me feel appreciative for every day of my life.

Sometimes I search for the purpose that this event might have brought to my life. Sometimes I search for the meaning and the lessons to be learned from it. Sometimes I could care less. They wanted the car, period. It had nothing to do with me. But that it happened had everything to do with my future. I could have been paralyzed by their provocative actions and dangerous behavior. Instead, I choose to pick up all of the puzzle pieces and gather all of them into a neat little pile. Once the pile is complete, I can put them into a beautiful sapphire jar and put it up on a shelf where I can access the event whenever I want. There, on the shelf, it can sit with all of my other experiences. If it's safely on that shelf, I can choose when to look at it, talk about it, and laugh about it. I can choose how it all affects me or not. It is mine. It is my past event. It has become a part of my experience and my history. I thank God and the universe for the opportunity to live and tell my story another day. Now, that's **Embrac**ing under the Smile From The Inside lifestyle.

The Day Manhattan Stood Still

When I look back at the events of September 11, 2011, even though it was over eleven years ago, it still is one of the clearest memories in all of my life. I will never forget the events that occurred on 9/11 nor will I ever forget many things about the long road back to normality and a regular routine in New York City. It has shaped me into the person I am today. It has most likely shaped everyone a little bit differently in my generation. It makes me think, though, that there are people that experience hatred and terror every day in the Middle East, certain parts of Africa and Asia, etc. How do these people handle those continuous actions of hate, sadness, and fear? I suppose living in that type of environment; it becomes a regular part of your existence, just like I saw in Mexico and in Ecuador. When I was in Ecuador, there were several strikes, tear-gas attacks, military coups, you know, the whole nine yards. It became a natural part of the day.

From the events of 9/11, I discovered that nothing unites a country and world like unprecedented and unfathomable terrorist attacks. In my opinion, Bush should have used 9/11 as a way to unite the world but, alas, he nor anyone around him could see the benefits of peace. They saw only politics, corruption, and revenge. Revenge is for the weak-minded people in this world, those who have not overcome their past. Revenge never works out well. It is the lowest energy vibration, down there with hatred and fear.

Character is not built through retaliation. Character is born through tireless reconciliation, compromise, and negotiations until blue in the face. Character is who you are, day after day, when all the odds are against you. It takes an enormous amount of courage to be who you are despite it all. That is the making of a man, a woman, and a human being. Sometimes all you can do is move on. Sometimes all you can do is smile. Sometimes all you can do is plan the biggest win-win all around. Focus on the previous steps, on your surrender, on your **Learning**. Don't focus on anyone else's. That is hugely important.

I used to think that by trying to teach someone else a lesson, that they would actually learn it. I have realized that that is *not* the case. On the one hand, we can say that it's just not worth the effort to try to teach someone a lesson, or that it's pointless because they will never learn. On the other hand, you can show them through exemplifying the good that lives inside you. I believe that people are ultimately good. I know sometimes it's hard to see, but when I am put to the test with the most challenging people, I see them as scared little children, living in fear. They apparently never quite got over the effects of an abused childhood or whatever traumatic experiences they feel they had. My job is to get to a place of compassion and sadness for that which they've become, and accept where they are.

I know that everyone can heal from his or her wounds. No matter how deep those events have penetrated, they can heal. One of my great lessons in this life is to not stay in a relationship with anyone who believes deep down that they cannot heal. It never works out. They must heal and love themselves at least 75% before letting anyone else love them and before they can give everything they can for the sake of a loving partnership. Coming full circle, those who seek revenge, seek hatred and fear. Those who seek peace, seek hope and love. It is that simple.

I believe in peace. I do not believe in war, at any cost. I feel like, in today's society and beyond, War is no longer the answer, ever. In the recently opened film, "Lincoln," there is an incredible line of dialogue. "Abe Lincoln" states that war is intimate and ugly. I could not have said that better myself. I believe that spending oodles of money on military defense is a tremendous waste and should be largely reduced. Instead, I believe the government should channel those funds and that energy into intelligence, conflict resolution, and the American education system. With more intelligence and constructive conversations in our schools, we are more likely to promote peace and communications.

I am a sucker for aliens-coming-to-Earth-type stories, fiction or alleged non-fiction. They usually portray the "aliens" to be hostile and wanting to take over the Earth. My theory is as follows: if there are extraterrestrials and they have found a way to travel at the speed of light, then they must have enough intelligence to know that peace is the way to build stronger allegiances and stronger galaxies. They would come in peace and probably speak to us telepathically, in our minds. If they have found a way to travel through time and space, they definitely would use more of their brains than we do. Whether or not we would be able to understand them is another story! My point here is that the more intelligent a species, a civilization, or a person, the more it or he realizes that peace is the only way to not just survive, but to thrive and go the farthest.

Similarly, teamwork is extremely important in most corporate America jobs. Do you know why? Teamwork is the way to conquer just about anything. This involves trust, a common understanding, listening, sharing, compassion, and friendship. The more we concentrate our focus on accomplishing our dreams, the more realistic and tangible they can become. The only way is through peace. At some point in my life, I hope the word "WAR" becomes a distant memory. I hope it becomes a word that no one uses anymore, unless for the purposes of discussing the history of Earth and **Learning** from our biggest mistakes.

I recently discovered that the most powerful concepts in this Universe are Hope and Love. *Without love, hope cannot exist.* Hope raises love to the maximum degree. If you look at all movies, especially the alien invasion ones, what keeps everyone going? Hope, right? Why do they have hope? Because they love their country. Because they love someone on the other side of those mountains. Because they need to protect their most precious commodity in life... that which and those whom they love. If you do not LOVE something or someone, then there is little hope for you. Love gives hope the unlimited power and strength one needs to overcome any situation. Love gives hope wings to fly. Ok, too esoteric, I know, but I was feeling it. Love ignites hope like nothing else. When all else fails, there is love and hope.

There's a reason why this concept exists in almost every single story on Earth.

Life can be, at times, an overwhelming cloud of fear and doubt. The trick is not to let life get to you. We all have times of fear and doubt, and we can all help ourselves out of it too. I know it sounds easier said than done, but if you focus on the great things in your life, and listen to your good feelings, those incredible feelings of goodness will eventually start to shift your emotions, and that's when the magic happens. That's when you can reach for the stars.

I only recently fully understood this concept. It took me thirty-three years to understand that a bad mood or a depressing couple of days can be turned around if you want it badly enough. It occurs when you continue to focus on those better feelings even when you are feeling down. Eventually, if you focus with all your might, you will experience a shift. It will work. Keep doing it, over and over again.

I'm still not very good at the above-mentioned technique… but I'm getting there. It's not too hard to think about that which sucks in your life… but how about practicing the opposite? What's going well in your life? When you try, you discover that it's also not that difficult to find great things in your life. Mine usually starts with my farm, Maggie, my nephew, my parents, my sister/aunt, then Maggie again (cause she brings me oodles of happy thoughts), and then I start to feel better little by little about whatever was just plaguing me. This is not a one-time exercise. No. This is an exercise that needs to be done perhaps five, ten, or twenty times prior to having any type of success. Even if it changes your mood for a second, that's a start. It's well worth it, though, to keep at it. You have my word.

9/11 may have help shaped who I am today, but it won't bring me down, and it won't bring this country down. There is a great deal to do. One of my missions in this world is to save the world. I don't quite know how I am going to accomplish this. Perhaps it is one person at a time, perhaps it will be thousands at a time. Either way, I feel like I am finally coming into my own. I have been on a quest since the age of five to figure out these feelings of wanting to save the world. That's when I wanted to be a fireman. I believe I am finally starting to see how to start. It starts with you, the reader, my audience.

A Friend Taken Too Young

Four weeks after my best friend Luli passed away, her sister contacted me and requested that I bring back to Ecuador a chest of Luli's clothes from the family in New Jersey that she lived with during her time in the New York area. You want me to do what??? Apparently, Luli had always planned on returning to the States to live. With that plan in mind, she left a chest full of clothes behind. It was suddenly my job to collect the chest, fly with it to Ecuador, and then go through the clothes with Luli's sister and mother.

Um… really? Wow. That's an odd request. Of course, I would do it. I would have done anything for Luli, Majo, and/or her family. Truth be told, from the moment I went to pick up the chest until the moment I went through the various clothing items with her family, I constantly felt the presence of Luli. Since I had already made my peace, this gave me great comfort. I knew that since I was asked to take care of her family, I would do so with my

love, my support, and my "forma de ser". (Remember this amazing expression in Spanish, unlike any expression in the English
language. Again, it literally means your "way of being", but it
goes so much further than that. It is you at your best and utmost
self-expression. It is the way you carry yourself and the way you
portray yourself to the world.) I knew I would have to use my
"forma de ser" to speak to this recently love-torn family. I knew
it wasn't going to be easy, but I had the utmost of faith and trust
in myself. Luli had trust in me too. Owning your "forma de ser"
and amazing light within are both signs of a person who Smiles
From The Inside.

Since Luli and Majo, in my mind, were a gift from God, I always
treated their family also as a gift from God. When I arrived at their
lovely but modest home, one week or so after retrieving the chest,
I was greeted with lots of love, lots of tears, and lots of happiness.
The house was almost exactly as I had remembered it. During my
crazy year in Ecuador, I would often venture over to the sisters'
house and write papers on their computer. We would make some
fantastic dinner, and then I would proceed to type for the next
several hours, sometimes into the wee hours of the night. It is
appropriate to tell you now that I am NOT a procrastinator, and
therefore I would stay up late several days before an assignment
was due. Anyway... the house was always full of laughter, love,
and warmth. Only one thing had changed. Obviously, the only
thing missing was Luli. Her mother wanted to go through the
clothes right away, but I persuaded her to wait a few hours on my
night of arrival before we delved into the goodness that was Luli.

Mamá Finita could not bear to wait any longer, so we finally went
upstairs and started unpacking her glorious chest. It was filled

with Luli's favorite clothes. Clothes that we all remembered with such fondness. Finita continued to cry the entire night, while Majo and I tried to get through the experience as respectfully, lovingly, and quickly as possible. Finita told me that I could keep any piece of clothing I wanted, in honor of my bringing the chest five thousand plus miles. I looked and looked and finally decided on her favorite scrunchy. It was a beautiful parade of colors and smelled just like her. Do you know I have kept that scrunchy with me for years and years... and, as a matter of fact, I still always have the scrunchy sitting in every workspace that I have had since her passing. It's my little way of honoring Luli forever in my working world. That scrunchy means the world to me. I love it with all my heart. Just last week, I moved it right next to my bed. It acts as the skirt to one of my favorite and oldest teddy bears.

One of the most beautiful compliments I have ever received came that very weekend down in Ecuador. I was sitting around with Majo and we were reminiscing about old times... the Sexuality and Attraction class we all attended together (which I probably could have taught), meeting the president of the LGBTQ organization, traveling to the Amazon and getting lost on the night walk, nicknames for my man-part, (I bet you all are curious now), and how we all met. We were convinced that it was fate or destiny that brought us together.

It was then that Majo started telling me a story. I knew that when I had first arrived in Ecuador in 1997, Luli and Mamá Finita had been fighting pretty hard core all of the time, which clearly affected the entire family. Petico, their father, was always in the middle too. Majo went on to tell me just how bad it was. Apparently, it had gotten so bad at points that Luli would threaten to move out and/or leave for good, and move in to her silly American boyfriend's apartment. No one in the family liked that guy anyway. She mentioned that it got so bad that even Petico was thinking about leaving too. Ugh. Clearly, it was a rough time in that family.

It was about that time that Majo started praying. Mamá Finita was definitely a religious and proud woman, but Majo was more of a free spirit like myself. Majo told me that she prayed then for the first time in a long time. She prayed for an angel. She asked that God send her someone or something that would help out their poor family. Majo looked at me intensely and told me that she wanted me to know that the day she prayed for the angel was two weeks before I first arrived in Ecuador. She said that she had told her mother and father this and that they both agreed that I was their angel. Majo said to me, "When you showed up in our lives, everything started to slowly improve. Luli and my mother started to get along. Petico was happier than ever and felt that the family would never return to that terrible time." There were tears in her eyes at this point. She said, "You were our angel!"

I was flabbergasted and honored and didn't know exactly to say. Sometimes silence is a great thing. No one had ever called me an angel before and it was pretty much beyond my comprehension as to what that really meant. She could see my utter **Shock** and just let me have that moment. If you know me, I used to have a very hard time accepting compliments... up until around that time. It was the first compliment in my life that I accepted fully and wholly. There are no words to describe how that made me feel. Even now, it gets me pretty choked up. I was and still am honored that she calls me their angel.

To make it even that much more incredible, Majo didn't stop there. Apparently, Luli had told her sometime after I had come into their lives that she too had wished for some type of miracle just about the time I arrived in Quito. That's where I lost it... completely. It was already a great deal to handle, the angel comment, but *miracle* too? I eventually accepted the notion... and it remains to this day, the absolute highest compliment anyone has ever paid me. Compliments really are the words of the highest power.

I truly believe that everything and everyone comes into your life for a season and a reason. I have often seen this displayed in my own life. People come in just about exactly when they need to step in... just as gracefully (or not so gracefully) as they leave your lives exactly when they need to leave. If we are lucky, we get two to three bosom buddies who will be with us throughout our entire lives and who will be there for us, no matter what. Those are true friends. Luli and Majo were bosom buddies to me. And Luli, wherever you are, I adore and love you with all of my heart. These bosom buddies stick with you for life and they accept you 100% for all of your faults, your exaggerations, and your idiosyncrasies. Bosom buddies ooze unconditional love, which is the most powerful of all loves. It can be the easiest and it can also be the most challenging of all the loves. I implore you all to think about who you unconditionally love and keep them close. Do everything you can to have unconditional loves!

Speaking of unconditional loves, I have **Embraced** Luli's death in many ways... and I still like to think I speak with her from time to time. I dream about her a lot. I like to think she tells me things and is my angel from beyond watching out for me. It gave a great deal of comfort to her family that I have connected with her since her passing. I know Luli has my back. I really feel her with me… I'd like to say always, but perhaps not.

It was definitely too young for her to die, and definitely not fair to the rest of us, but her death has taught me a great deal about suffering. Apparently, she suffered silently for a few years with a couple grave secrets. Who knows what they are? No one should carry ANY secret burdens all by themselves. Luli was a happy and strong gal. Sometimes I wish I had been closer with her toward the end and sometimes I wish I could have done something to have prevented her death. At the end of the day, I had played my purpose in her life and played the most incredible role of the miracle in her existence.

She will forever live in my heart and forever be with me as I journey on. I think she gets a kick out of my life… and stays around because there's never a dull moment. I fully **Embrace** her death as a reminder that people die, young and old, every day. Each day we wake up, we should be grateful to wake up, live, and breathe another day on this wonderful place we call Earth. Apparently, elderly people also make those comments a lot. It can't all be hogwash!

5 THINGS TO REMEMBER WHEN IN EMBRACE

1. Appreciate and Forgive!

Without going through that event, I would not be where I am today. Appreciate the experience. Be grateful for the chance to overcome yet another obstacle on your path to Smiling From The Inside. Learn to Forgive. Forgive someone else. Forgive yourself. Forgive someone else. Forgive yourself. Forgive someone else. Forgive yourself. Any questions?

2. Remember the Law of Attraction.

Think better thoughts. The Law of Attraction states: that which is like unto itself, is drawn... To better understand the Law of Attraction, see yourself as a magnet attracting unto you the essence of that which you are thinking and feeling. And so, if you are feeling fat, you cannot attract thin. If you feel poor, you cannot attract prosperity, and so on.

3. Be Careful What You Choose.

With every choice, whether simple or complex, you have the capacity to change the entire course of the rest of your life. Think about it... every choice you make can lead you in a completely different direction. You are the apparent ruler of your destiny... well... you and God, the Universe, Jesus, whatever you wish. Make the impossible, possible. Choose a different choice.

4. Celebrate Who You Are!

You are your biggest fan. No one will champion you more than you. Love who you are. Celebrate who you are! Celebrate the little things! Celebrate the big things! Take yourself out and celebrate who you are and who you have become!

5.   The Best is Yet to Come.

Let your gifts shine. Always believe that something wonderful is about to happen. Be excited about your future, after all, your light will always be greater than your past.

EMBRACE – In Conclusion:

"**Yeehaw!**" - Move over Acceptance, it's all about **Embrace**. Acceptance is defined as the "willingness to tolerate a difficult or unpleasant situation."[12] Once you have accepted the realities of the situation, you are one half-step away from **Embrace**. I believe that accepting the circumstances of any situation is just not enough and it's only going part of the way and doing part of the work. While acceptance is a great gateway to the deeper level of healing, when you **Embrace** a situation, you are setting yourself free from the attachments to it. You are also literally giving a hug to the issue prior to letting it go. You appreciate that this event has happened and you understand that it's part of your history and is now a part of you. Finally, it has helped you to become the person you are today. For without it, you would not be the same person you are today. It is a clear and peaceful place. It means that tomorrow is a brand new day. All characters welcome!

Everything in life is a choice. We can change the course of our lives with every new choice that comes our way. We can choose to **Embrace** everything that is given to us in our lives or we can choose to fight it. I believe that the Universe/God does not give us more than we can handle. Sometimes, I know, I have my doubts, but in the end, we can overcome anything.

We make choices all of the time that can and will affect our lives. Choose everything wisely. For me, I find that the big decisions in life may require that I take some time to ponder and weigh the options. The clear path is pretty much always an intuitive

---

12   "Acceptance," OxfordDictionary.com, 2012.

decision for me. In other words, when I close my eyes, take a few deep breaths, and listen to my inner voice, the decision always becomes clear. (Whereas, let's not even talk about restaurant menus! It takes me forever to make a decision!)

Clearly, we have fate and destiny that gracefully shine into our lives and gracefully dim out of our lives. But I would argue that everything in our lives is a choice - yes, everything - our lives and the success of our lives are pretty well created by us. For example, I did not choose to be almost kidnapped, but I did choose to take a director role in Mexico that potentially could put me in harm's way, right? I made a series of choices that led me to that spot, that day. I'm not saying I caused it to happen, but I certainly made enough choices to place me then and there in that terrifying situation. Therefore, our lives are both the sum total of our choices combined with the random cards (or not so random) the universe deals us. And I choose how to deal with this almost kidnapping each and every day. I can be okay with what happened or I can choose to be sad and depressed about it. What I'm really trying to say here is the choice to live gracefully or live miserably is yours and yours alone. So, live gracefully and happily!

When I learned this ultimate lesson - that everything in my life is a choice - the whole responsibility of my life, I felt, fell on my shoulders. It was a LOT of pressure. I can definitely take responsibility for most of the actions and/or behaviors in my life, but the thought of each and every choice having a repercussion was a bit too much to handle. I decided to sit with that thought and just be with it for a few days. It took about three to four days to sink in. It is overwhelming to learn, but once you have grasped the concept, you can see that the possibilities and opportunities are endless. By the way, in case you are wondering, I have not mastered living like this 100% of the time. Not even close. I strive for excellence and I strive for the where-withal one day to walk this path every moment of every day. As with everything else and as I've said time and time again, life is a work in progress and growth is a forever-changing update to our current existence.

Believe in happiness. Believe in inner peace. Believe in content-ment. Believe in something. I know it is all easier said than done. But try it anyway. If you do all of this, I guarantee your light will shine and you will Smile From The Inside.

In yoga, Savasana is specifically designed to occur at the end of each yoga class. After all of the hard work, the focus, and the unbelievable perseverance you give in the class, Savasana is the gateway back to the real world. It is a time for silent reflec-tion where all prior exercises, conditioning, practice, mistakes, and mental as well as physical exhaustion culminate into one final experience – **Embrace**. As the class ends, there is no feeling quite so expansive, or so peaceful. It feels like you are on top of the world. It feels like you are Smiling From The Inside.

At any moment, we can choose to **Embrace** the hiccups, the bad stuff, and the tragic events, just as we **Embrace** the accom-plishments, the good stuff, and the fantastic events. Many of us, without thinking, choose to go down the same path as always, expecting different results. If you keep doing what you've always done, you'll keep getting what you've always gotten. Be differ-ent. Be you! Shine! The bottom line - if you learn nothing else from this book - is **Embrace Life**. **Embrace** you. **Embrace** who you are. Grow. Live. Learn. Smile.

You have been diligent. You have been patient. You have done a LOT of work on yourself. Everything that came before makes sense now, doesn't it? Without the four preceding stages, **Shock**, **Mock-cceptance**, **In Overwhelmdom**, and **Learning**, **Embrace** would simply not be possible. This is the icing on the cake, the cherry on top of the amazing Neapolitan sundae. **Embrace** makes it easier to be happier, to feel joy and to enjoy every day. Hence, it is the last step to mastering the little challenges presented to you in this life. In doing so, you will feel alive, energized, appreciative, and content. Welcome to Smiling From The Inside.

S.M.I.L.E. METHOD
THE RE-CAP

I have thrown a great deal of information at you, so let's take another look at some of the main points.

Shock - "Whoa!" - is a natural, physical and emotional reaction to surprising and upsetting experiences. It is the body's way of saying, "Yo, hold up! What just happened?" or "What did you just say to me?" or just plain "What???" **Shock** is the necessary pause we need in order to handle whatever situation has presented itself. Just like in yoga, **Shock** is similar to warming up the body and focusing on your breath in order to prepare the mind and body for the extreme. It is the first important step we all must take to live a more authentic, more content, and more solid presence on this Earth.

Mock-cceptance - "I'm Fine!" - is part-denial and part-acceptance. Hence, **Mock-cceptance**. It really does feel like you may be on top of the world. It gives you the false sense of security that everything is A-okay, even though everything is heightened around you because your mind and body are going through something big. They are dealing with it the only way they know how. Trust that your mind, body, and soul know what they are doing. After all, they have thousands of years of evolution behind them. **Mock-cceptance** is like the Sun Salutations in Yoga. Even though you have done these exercises a million times, you are conditioning your body from the inside. This is where the juices start flowing in the class, and similarly, in your life. Thus, it's the second necessary step we all must overcome to live an easier Smile From The Inside way of life.

In Overwhelmdom - "Ugh!" - is the culmination of personal and unique individual emotions. It is a hypersensitivity to all that goes on around you. Don't be surprised if you really have no patience to listen to anyone else's drama. Anything can happen and every possible feeling will and does come up. It is the part where the real work is about to begin and your mind, body, and soul are preparing you for the task at hand – healing. This is the part of the yoga class when you are sweating profusely, breathing for your life, and you really just don't think you can hold the pose for another FOUR breaths. It feels impossible. However, if you stick with it, you will feel accomplished, proud, and a huge sense of empowerment. It is the key step to the overall adjustment that is imminently going to happen within your life. Thus, it's the third important step we all must conquer to live a more balanced and more centered Smile From The Inside life.

Learning - "Ohhh... Wow!" - is where you surrender yourself to the way things are, right now, in the present. This is the hardest part of the journey because it is not about taking control of the situation. It is about understanding how to "be" with the situation. **Learning** is how we know that the worst is over and it's now time to get up, move on, and live life to the fullest. **Learning** to surrender happens when one is present enough to see the situation from a non-biased perspective and to see one's role and responsibility therein. Without the acknowledgement and validation of your situation at hand, you cannot proceed to the next step - **Embrace**. In yoga, the key to arm balances is full body memory. In other words, amidst all the mistakes, the falls, the "almost theres," finally, one day it just clicks, and the body remembers how to reconstruct the position naturally. It remembers what to do and what not to do. **Learning** from your mistakes is a wonderful way to retain valuable information. It can be what differentiates you from the rest of the individuals around you. Thus, it's the second-to-last step we all must surmount to live a more comfortable and more insightful Smile From The Inside life.

Embrace - "Yeehaw!" - is to accept without judgment, to accept without fear, and to accept with love and grace. Embracing goes much further than just accepting. It is the celebration of you, who you are now, where you've come from, and where you are going. Some issues may take longer to heal than others, and that's okay, too. It is when you can appreciate that this event has happened and you understand that it's more than just part of your history, it is now a part of you. This event has helped you to become the person you are today. Like yoga's Savasana, it is a time for silent reflection where all prior exercises, conditioning, practice, mistakes, and mental as well as physical exhaustion culminate into one final experience – **Embrace**. It feels that everything in the world is right and just plain good. It feels like you are Smiling From The Inside.

THE BEST IS YET TO COME

AWARENESS IS KEY. Awareness is the key to healing. Awareness will set you apart from the rest. So, be aware of your patterns. Be aware of your own sensitive points. Please also try to be aware of those around you. **Learning** to be aware of your own process is of the utmost importance. **Learning** to identify your own healing stages will allow you a great reprieve and understanding of what to expect. We all like to witness repetition and we all like to have an idea of what to expect, especially if it's going to hurt physically or emotionally.

Through my twelve years of practicing yoga, as well as a yoga teacher training course at Om Yoga Center in New York, I learned that one of the major purposes of yoga is to help one breathe easier during any unexpected, traumatic, or sad event. The concept is that you (the yogi) have consistently pushed through literally thousands of tight squeezes, spaces, and poses. You have prepared and conditioned the appropriate mental, physical, and spiritual stamina/response to help guide you through all the unforeseen and tough moments. Between conditioning and recognizing your patterns, you will make your journey easier and more manageable - the purpose of the Smile From The Inside approach.

When I speak about unforeseen, traumatic, or unexpected events, in the end, they are all just euphemisms for dealing with hurt or pain. Pain is the physical suffering from injury or disease experienced through the central nervous system. Its purpose is to alert the body to damage or danger to its system.[13] Hurtful and painful events will happen just like there will be ups and there will be downs. Terrible and unfortunate things happen all of the time, to us all. At their core, they are emotionally charged "events" that, with our conditioning, practice, and awareness, we can empower ourselves to deal with head on, in a healthy, productive, and efficient manner.

In spite of all the modern-day distractions and over-stimulation available nowadays, it is hard to just allow our human minds and bodies to do what they need to do in order to survive and acquiesce to the event at hand. I believe that the human capacity to heal is one of the most amazing, complex, and misunderstood phenomena of our time. Remember, we can heal from anything. We can heal from everything. All we need is courage, hope, and love.

---

13   Beins, Bernard, Feldman, Alan J., and Gall, Susan, *The Gale Encyclopedia of Psychology*, Gale, 1996.

LIFE GETS IN THE WAY. Life always gets in the way. Since I started writing this, even more sad and unfortunate events have happened in my life experience, which almost prevented me from finishing this book. Instead, however, I used those experiences as additional inspiration to complete it. Perfection is not something I seek. I am human and make mistakes just like everybody else. Albert Einstein wisely commented, "I have to be willing to give up what I think I am in order to become what I will be." We must get out of our own way in order to grow and heal.

SOMETIMES YOU GET IN THE WAY. I wish everyone could see who he or she is, clearly, from an objective standpoint, and be aware of how one's past behaviors affect the present. I also wish everyone could see how the current learned actions, behaviors, and habits from the past can be changed in the present with a great deal of effort. Sometimes you just need to get out of your own way. This is my hope for the world.

HEALING. The lines are always blending between the steps of healing. One is inevitably bound to another, which is bound to another, and so on and so forth. This process is messy by natural design. It throws you off your normality and thrusts you into a world of confusion and absorption. Healing keeps you safe when you need to be kept safe, and keeps you strong when you fear all else is wrong. Life has the uncanny capability of throwing as much as can be thrown at once. Some of us are dealt a sour hand for the formative and "imprintive" (wink) early years, and some of us are dealt a sour hand in the formative and lasting elder years. I wholeheartedly believe that we can heal from all of these unfortunate events and/or wounds. Think of the stories you can share afterwards, and the people you can inspire and encourage.

It's more work than most of us are willing to do, but it is possible. All things are possible.

The more challenging the obstacles, the more rewarding the life in the end, I guarantee it. No matter who you are, or where you are in your life, events will happen that will overcome you with fear, doubt, worry, etc. Take a few breaths. For me, by the time I was twenty-four, I felt like I had experienced more in my short life than most people do in their entire lives. Now that I'm in my early thirties, I have lived a lifetime of great stories. Perhaps one day I'll write about some of the others, but for now, just do me one favor and inspire one person to Smile From The Inside every day.

THE BEST IS YET TO COME. After the **Shock** subsides, the reality morphs into **Mock-cceptance**. After the emotions **In Overwhelmdom** run their course and **Learning** settles the unsettled emotions, you will find that with each passing day, life gets a little bit easier and a little bit better. Finally, when you **Embrace** the situation fully, the once impossibly gynormous waves now ease themselves to calm, and the space will open for the next best thing in your life. Lastly, always, always remember, the best is yet to come. *Your* best is yet to come!

You have worked through the concept of healing through S.M.I.L.E. and you have listened to my personal experiences. I never said the five phases were easy. Everyone's healing process is slightly different. If you are mindful of everything we have covered, your life will become easier. If you are grappling to uncover which step you are in the process of, go back, flip through the pages, and identify your respective stage. I want you to become aware of your own process. If you weren't aware before, I have now given you the tools to an increased sense of awareness. Unfortunately, I cannot do the work for you, so that's your job. You must put in the time. You must do the hard work every day. You will get through whatever it is you are going through.

Life isn't quite as easy it we think is, but it *is* easier than we believe it could be. As you know, I believe that everything in life is a choice. In an instant, we can always choose differently and thereby change the course of our lives. I believe that heaven and hell are right here on Earth. We can either choose to live in HEAVEN or choose to live in HELL. We all venture back and forth. You choose... heaven or hell?

Remember, feeling is a good thing. It means that you are alive. It means that you can change. It means that you are capable of great things. *I contend that all we need in this world is LOVE and HOPE.* Unconditional love is really the only love situation that works on this Earth. I wish we all could experience it over and over again.

Hope is the only emotion that will keep us going even when all other lights have gone out, even when there is no end in sight, and the world is ending. Hope is what keeps us going each and every day. Never forget that hope is just as powerful as love. Love and hope are the two things that every great epic hero has, in any tale, romance, thriller, comedy or grandiose tragedy - the protagonist always prevails with the help of love and hope.

I'll leave you with this: I believe that with love and hope, all events labeled as traumatic can be healed. It will not be easy, but it can be done. Sometimes we win. Sometimes we lose. Never lose hope - the best is always yet to come.

Congratulations! Now you can Smile From The Inside too! I am sure that by now, a new you has begun to surface. Allow it to happen. It could be the best thing you have ever done for yourself.

SMILE FROM THE INSIDE

SMILE FROM THE INSIDE

adjective

1. Centered; knowing who you are, celebrating who you are, and radiating peace.

2. Authentic; endeavoring to be yourself at every moment, even in the darkest of situations.

3. Unfazed; not letting things bother you too much, letting the bigger things and smaller things roll off your back.

verb

1. *To Allow / Enable; to empower and motivate others around you. Just by being around you, your way of being will inspire others to be better and encourage them to do more.*

2. *To be grateful; to strive for appreciation and acknowledgement of everything you have and everything you have been given.*

3. *To reframe; to act as an intuitive individual who inspires and encourages others to shift limited views, actions, and / or behaviors, by dealing with the past, healing in the present, and reeling into the future.*

noun

1. *Awareness; cognizance of your past, present, and future; and through knowledge gained, ability to shift your emotions, perceptions, and hence your life.*

2. *An individual who always has hope and love in his or her eyes.*

3. *An individual who carries an incredible amount of light inside.*

What does it mean, to Smile From the Inside? People who Smile From the Inside are those who, when they smile, their way of being shines through so brightly, it is impossible not to notice the depth, the hope, and the happiness within. The majority of the time, you will not only see the truth, giving, and joy but also the enthusiastic life energy, motivation, and empowerment through their smile alone.

Whenever anyone meets me, the most common comment I receive is that I am a "breath of fresh air." That's what Smiling From The Inside is. No matter what happens, you still carry a light load. Smiling From The Inside is about finding the good feelings, finding the positive wherever you can. It's about living authentically and being you 100% of the time - even when it's tough. It's about being scared, yet being fearless enough to plunge through it regardless.

You know you are a person who Smiles From The Inside when you feel more alive and energized all of the time, feel a greater sense of balance, and feel more comfortable with yourself and your surroundings. You will be amazed at how things fall into place and start shifting to where you want them to be, because you are enthusiastically willing it to be so.

If you have recently experienced something traumatic, you can't just jump into this way of being. You will go through a process of healing that can bring you to a better place. Following the S.M.I.L.E. approach, being patient with yourself, and giving time its due will help you to heal.

My vision in this world is to inspire the world, one by one, to Smile From The Inside. I want others to know happiness and contentment. I want you to know the passion, light, and enthusiasm that exist within all of us. I hope that you look for gifts from the universe, live on gifted time, and intimately connect with friends, loved ones, and animals. Once we get out of our own way, not only are all things possible, but we also allow ourselves the ability to dream, imagine, and play with life. Now, go inspire the world to Smile From The Inside, be fruitful, and make me proud!

The End.

ACKNOWLEDGEMENTS

I would like to remember all those loved ones lost: Luli, Linda, Buster, Vinnie, Max, and Santiago. You each shined brightly and exemplified what it means to Smile From The Inside. I will never forget you.

Everyone who has helped me in this journey we call life from preschool to elementary, and from junior high to my three years in high school. Thank you to all of the wonderful teachers in my life, including Ms. Daisy, Mr. Prescott, Ms. Rankin, and Trudeau.

I would like to give a shout out to my Promax peeps: Sonia, Belinda (and their amazing husbands), Stephen, Juan Carlos, Michael, etc.... for without you, it would have been impossible to get through those few months of cancer. You were my rock and my family and you have my utmost respect and esteem.

To friends of my seasoned past: Jason, Rosemary Saggio, Stacey, Ciara and fam, Michelle, Froh, Gabriel, Rosie, Erin, Heather, Annika, Jaime, Erik, Liz Feliz, and Majo. I would also like to recognize the newer ones coming along for the journey: Duane, Ryan, Timmy, Shane, Heather, Belle, Andrea, Renata, Cathy, the Julies, the Wootens (possibly my biggest fans), and all of my former and all of my current neighbors.

Maggie, I love and adore each and every hair of your furry little Frenchie body. To my gay fabulous backyard, I salute my "visiting" Nigerian dwarf dairy goats, Vinnie and Trixie, as well as my four hens (in pecking order): Griselda, Daisy, Grandma Sparkle, and Tilda. Butter Ball...RIP.

I could not have made it through the last couple of years without my LP60 peeps: Tracy, Benjamin, Diann, Liz, Corrina, Chad, et al. Love you all and wishing you nothing but the best. And a shout out to LP61, 62, 63 and all LPs to come.

My intimate family who has put up with my craziness over the past thirty-some-odd years: Shayna, Ross, Miles Benjamin, Aunty, Maine, Samantha, and Derek... and the rest of the Santoro and Shulman/Cohen clans. Shout out to my Quito Family, my Toronto and Montreal family, my Los Angeles family, my New York family, and my second moms along the way: Beth, Barbara, Mama Pepita, Mama Finita, and Gomi. You are forever in my hearts, thoughts, and prayers.

I want to take a moment to thank Joe Marich. I sincerely hope that your candor, honesty, and pure infotainment pay off for the both of us. Thank you so much for all of your patience, seeing my potential, and giving me the tools to figure it all out on my own.

I also must thank my incredible and oh-so-honest editor, Jennifer Norian, for all of her time, energy, and patience reading my manuscript over and over again. Thank you! And thank you Katie, Kim, and Andrea for your thoughts and support as well. There's definitely more to come!

Look Tori, Lynnie, and Stacey, I am enough. I am worth it.

Last, I would like to acknowledge the most recent love in my life, Adam. I appreciate all of the work we have done together and look forward to a long life of love, spontaneity, drama, and close friendship. xoxo.

ABOUT THE AUTHOR

Seth Santoro is a life coach, yogi, writer, blogger, public speaker, aspiring TV host, and producer. His vision is to inspire the world, one by one, to Smile From The Inside. He has a great deal to say, the basis of which is: *know* who you are and BE who you are - no matter what the circumstance or your past - and you can heal from anything.

Born and raised in New England, educated and developed in New York City, nurtured and groomed in Los Angeles, Seth Santoro carries within him a unique and never-seen-before force with which to be reckoned. He one day plans to have his own TV talk show, one that combines Oprah's integrity and empowerment, Andy Cohen's chutzpah, Ellen's humor and freshness, Anderson Cooper's sparkle, Ryan Seacrest's superb star hosting quality and, finally, the Clintons' charisma. But for now, he will just have to be known as the "Smile From The Inside" guy.

Seth currently lives in Los Angeles, with his partner, Adam, his four hens, his two "visiting" goats: Vincent Van Goat and Trixie Van Goat, and his Frenchie, Maggie.

For Speaking engagements, Private Coaching sessions, and more, please visit either www.SethSantoro.com or www.SmileFromTheInside.com. Or check out Seth's "Smile From The Inside" blog at http://smilefromtheinside24.blogspot.com.

UPCOMING TITLES FROM THE AUTHOR

HOW I CONTINUED TO SMILE FROM THE INSIDE... EVEN IN MEXICO

(SUMMER 2013)

In an obscure and mind-blowing journey plagued with lawyers, lemons, lesbians, and lazy cartels, this nonfiction personal narrative recounts one O.C.D. gay man's fascinating and authentic experience of living and working in Mexico. Seth Santoro presents a first-hand account of his everyday struggles while immersed in this extraordinary culture, amidst both the kindest and the most treacherous of Mexican people. If you want the whole almost kidnapping story, the detailed account of Silvestre's Express Kidnapping, and know more about Seth's crazy and dangerous run-ins with cartels and gun-toting assassins, you'll enjoy reading his second book, *How I Continued to Smile From the Inside... Even in Mexico.*

How You Can Learn To Smile From The Inside
(Winter 2014)

There are so many events from childhood that burden us and play out daily in our present lives. What if there was a solid way to help you work through past hurts and experiences? What if there was an approach to help you better process the past, to have a much more fulfilling and incredible present? In Seth Santoro's third book, *How You Can Learn To Smile From The Inside,* he outlines his G.R.A.C.E. Method for how to heal the mind and soul from childhood trauma. Interwoven in this how-to-heal guide are stories of incredible heroism, strength, and courage, as told by outstanding individuals who did just that: freed themselves from the residual burdens carried within from disturbing childhood experiences. *How You Can Learn To Smile From The Inside* is the third book in the Smile From The Inside series, and Healing is guaranteed.

If you think you have an incredible story that needs to be told, contact me! I'm still accepting the stories of silent heroes. I might just put your story in my next book!

The Transformist
(Autumn 2014)

A fictional novel about a displaced child who rejuvenates the human spirit and saves the world, one person at a time.

72525530R10146

Made in the USA
San Bernardino, CA
26 March 2018